CW00821101

OPERATION MOSES

OPERATION MOSES

THE STORY OF THE EXODUS
OF THE FALASHA JEWS
FROM ETHIOPIA

Tudor Parfitt

WEIDENFELD AND NICOLSON LONDON

For Justin and Natasha

Printed in Great Britain by
Butler & Tanner Limited
Frome and London

Contents

Illustrations

Two cartoons by Dosh which appeared in *Ma'ariv*, January 1985 (© *Dosh*)

An Israeli welcomes an elderly Ethiopian Jew, January 1985 (*Associated Press*)

Young Falashas demonstrating in Jerusalem against symbolic conversion, January 1985 (*photo: Jim Hollander, Popperfoto*)

A young Falasha girl in Israel, February 1985 (© *Tudor Parfitt*)

A Falasha couple in their flat in a government absorption centre (© *Raissa Page/Format*)

Acknowledgements

A few days after Operation Moses started, I arrived in Sudan to gather material on the Falashas for a Minority Rights Group report and to continue researching a book for Weidenfeld and Nicolson on Jewish communities throughout the world. Shortly after my return Lord Weidenfeld suggested I write this book and my first thanks, therefore, go to him. I am grateful for the friendship and assistance given to me by the Falashas I met in Sudan and Israel. Much of the material in this book is based on conversations with officials of international relief organizations, journalists, diplomats and Sudanese and Israeli officials. For obvious reasons their names must go unrecorded. I would like to acknowledge the assistance in various forms of the following: Dr David Appleyard, Mr Peter Brod, Mr Karel Gardosh (Dosh), Dr Arthur Irvine, 'Joshua', Mr David Kessler, Dr David Patterson, Mrs Lola Singer, Mr Robert Straus, Mr Arieh Turchan, Professor Edward Ullendorff, and Mr Ben Whitaker; also the information departments of the Israeli Embassy in London and the Board of Deputies of British Jews, the library staffs of the Institute of Jewish Affairs, London, the Kressel Library, Oxford, and the Library of the School of Oriental and African Studies, London. I am most grateful to Miss Naomi Francis for typing the manuscript. Mr Julian Hale spurred me on mercilessly and gave much needed advice. The clear-minded and cheerful editorial criticism of Miss Linda Osband has been invaluable. My greatest thanks go to my wife Mája, without whose encouragement and massive tolerance this book would not have been written.

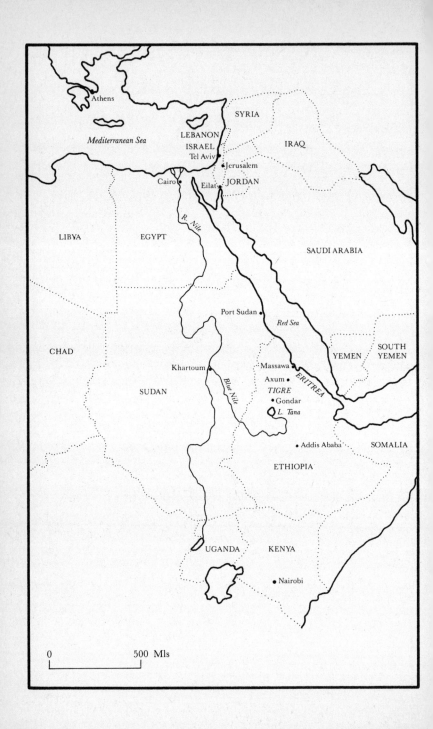

Athens

Mediterranean Sea

SYRIA

LEBANON
ISRAEL
Tel Aviv

IRAQ

Jerusalem

Cairo

Eilat

JORDAN

LIBYA

EGYPT

R. Nile

SAUDI ARABIA

Port Sudan

Red Sea

CHAD

Khartoum

Massawa

YEMEN

SOUTH
YEMEN

Axum

ERITREA

TIGRE

Gondar

L. Tana

Blue Nile

SUDAN

Addis Ababa

SOMALIA

ETHIOPIA

UGANDA

KENYA

Nairobi

0   500 Mls

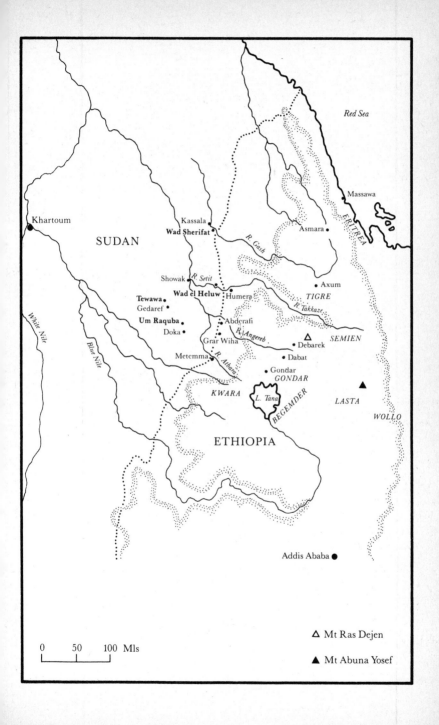

Red Sea

Massawa

Khartoum

SUDAN

Kassala
Wad Sherifat

Asmara

ERITREA

R. Gash

Showak
R. Setit

Axum

Tewawa
Wad el Heluw Humera
Gedaref

TIGRE

R. Takkaze

Um Raquba
Doka

Abderafi
R. Angereb

SEMIEN

Grar Wiha
Metemma
R. Atbara

△ Debarek

Dabat

Gondar
GONDAR

▲

KWARA

L. Tana

BEGEMDER

LASTA

WOLLO

White Nile

Blue Nile

ETHIOPIA

Addis Ababa ●

0   50   100 Mls

△ Mt Ras Dejen

▲ Mt Abuna Yosef

'Deliver me and put me with Thy people Israel, for Thou art just, O Lord.'

A FALASHA PRAYER

CHAPTER ONE

Sabbath in Tewawa

The rutted track out of Gedaref was baked black and hard by the sun. At the edge of the road, burning refuse smoked against the afternoon sky. Storks picked through the rubble. Was there anything edible in Gedaref's rubbish tips? A thin boy watched the birds intently.

I was in the back of a decrepit box-car, which was taking Ethiopian refugees back from Gedaref to their camp. The truck hit a pot-hole and swayed dangerously. One of the men fell against me. He seemed to weigh nothing. Everyone was silent. We reached the top of a small hill and I could see the plain stretching into the distance. Before the drought this had been good land. Now it was desert littered with stones and torn plastic bags. Tewawa refugee camp overlooks this sea of desolation.

For years refugees have crossed from Ethiopia into eastern Sudan. In Tewawa the Ethiopians used to make a living working for local Sudanese farmers. Then came the drought. Now 20,000 people live here without work and without hope. Tewawa has become a permanent township of hundreds of *tukuls* (dome-shaped grass huts), each one surrounded by thorn hedges and bare patches of land which may once have been vegetable patches. Smoke rose from cooking fires, but there was no smell of food.

Dawit, an Eritrean student who was serving as my guide and interpreter, told me we had arrived. 'It is a dangerous place. As many people are knifed every night as die of hunger.' The central square of the camp was teeming with people. A hundred or so men stood in one corner selling things. One had a shirt, another a pair of trousers, another a skirt. Those with nothing to sell pushed their way feverishly through the crowd. 'Most of the fights are over women,' Dawit continued. 'There are many prostitutes here.'

We passed a few drunken men standing outside a couple of *tukuls* that served as a brothel. From the door of one of the huts two girls of striking beauty watched us walk by. On the other side of the brothel we saw a man lying on the ground, blood pouring out of a deep gash on his leg. He was singing. 'He has been drinking *tedj*. The war widows make it and sell it, but the Sudanese police punish them if they find them out. They get thirty lashes and three months in prison.' Since the introduction of Islamic law (*Sharia*) in 1983, alcohol has been banned in Sudan. 'The old women make *tedj* and the young women are whores. They have to make a living.' Dawit looked embarrassed.

We were walking down a wide path bordered by thorn hedges. The *tukuls* on both sides were adorned with crosses. I asked Dawit if all the refugees were Christians. 'I am a Christian,' he said, pulling out a brass cross from beneath his shirt. 'Most of the refugees here are Christians but there are some Muslims too. We also have some Israelites.' He stumbled over the word. 'Did you know that there are Jews in Ethiopia? We call them Falashas but they call themselves Beta Israel – the House of Israel.'

It was the Falashas I had come to see on behalf of the Minority Rights Group. According to many reports, these Ethiopian Jews had fled persecution and famine in Ethiopia only to find themselves persecuted in the camps by the other Ethiopian refugees and regarded with suspicion by the Muslim Sudanese who administered the camps. There had even been reports that the Falashas were being poisoned. Terrified of their neighbours, they would never identify themselves as Jews.

'We do not like these people. They do very bad things to Christians. They brought the famine to Ethiopia. They killed Jesus.' Dawit scowled piously towards the only brick building in the camp – a white-washed Ethiopian church surrounded by a luxuriant garden. He was joined by some friends. 'That is the city of the Jews,' one of them said, pointing at a group of *tukuls* even more pitiful and derelict than the ones I had seen in the Christians' quarter. I asked them why these huts were worse than those further up the hill. 'They don't fix the *tukuls*. They are not staying here. They are going to Port Sudan and from there, by German boat, to the Jewish country, Israel. Two nights ago some went. Tonight some will go. The Falashas have got Israel. What have we Christians got?' He gestured hopelessly at the surrounding camp.

Dawit and I walked on towards the Falasha section of Tewawa. In the main alley there were a few groups of Falashas who looked at us suspiciously. No one spoke. For the most part they were dressed in cast-offs: once fashionable bell-bottomed trousers and long-collared shirts collected by relief organizations in the affluent West. The older men wore the Ethiopian cloak, the *shamma*. The men looked hostile and worried, but the children seemed excited as if they were waiting for something. The women were sitting in groups in front of their *tukuls*. Because of the Jewish Sabbath the cooking fires were not burning.

I decided to send Dawit back to the main square to wait for me there. He did not seem reluctant to go. A large crowd of children gathered round smiling and pulling at my shoulder-bag. The Sabbath, which finishes at sunset, was drawing to a close. I greeted them with the traditional Falasha blessing, '*Sanbat Salam*' – 'Sabbath Peace'. The men looked at me stonily, but one or two of the boys laughed and replied in Hebrew, '*Shalom.*' I said a few words in Hebrew. A tall teenage boy took me to one side and whispered to me in Hebrew, pointing at Dawit's retreating back: 'Be careful. That man is bad. You cannot trust him. Hundreds of us are going to Israel, but you must not tell anyone. We are leaving tonight.'

Sudan is still officially at war with Israel. How could the Falashas be going there from a rigidly Islamic, Arab League state? How was it that Sudan's State Security, the *Amnul-Dawla*, reputedly the best secret service in black Africa, was unaware of what was happening? Was this a clandestine Israeli operation like the Entebbe mission or were the

Sudanese themselves involved in some way? If the story got out, how would the other Arab states react? And if the Sudanese and the *AmnulDawla* were involved, why were there such poor security arrangements in Tewawa? If I could uncover this story, so could the dozens of Western journalists who were in Sudan reporting on the famine. At this point in my reverie, the sight of two armed men at the end of the dusty track assured me that the security arrangements were perhaps better than I thought. Ducking behind a *tukul* I made my way back to where Dawit was waiting for me in Tewawa's main square. We jumped into a box-car and returned to Gedaref. Before we got out he said, 'These camps are not refugee camps – they are concentration camps. I've been here for three years. Unlike the Jews, the rest of us will never get out.'

That night I drove back to Khartoum. Before continuing my investigations among the Falashas certain questions needed to be answered. I had stumbled on an extraordinary operation and I had to find out who was behind it. Before leaving London I had been briefed by an organization that monitors the situation of Jewish communities under threat. I had been given the telephone numbers of a few contacts in Khartoum. Perhaps one of them would be able to help.

The following morning I arranged to meet 'Joshua' on the terrace of the Grand Hotel overlooking the Blue Nile. I briefly mentioned the report I was planning to write on the Falashas and what I had discovered in Tewawa. He looked at me searchingly. Speaking slowly, in heavily accented English, he said: 'I am very sorry you found out. This is a top-secret operation. The *AmnulDawla* agents in Gedaref are supposed to have the whole place sealed off. If just one word of this gets to the press the operation is finished. These people will be left to rot in the camps. Hundreds have already died. Hundreds, perhaps thousands, will certainly die if we don't get them out. If you are wondering what the difference is between the Falashas and the thousands of other Ethiopians who are dying in the camps in the east, I'll tell you. Like me, the Falashas are Jews. But that is not the main difference. The Christian and Muslim refugees from Ethiopia cannot escape the famine and the camps because they have nowhere to go. No country will take them. During my lifetime, Jews have not always had the chance to escape when faced with destruction. This time, because Israel is prepared to take them, these black Jews do have a chance. If this story gets out the Falashas lose that chance.'

Joshua's real name and identity cannot be revealed. He is still in Khartoum and will stay there as long as Falashas cross from Ethiopia to Sudan looking for a way to get to Israel. He is a brave man, but on that November morning in Khartoum he was frightened: in part for himself, but most of all for the 10,000 people who for the next few weeks would be his responsibility. Joshua was the chief co-ordinator in Khartoum of Operation Moses.

A number of Israeli agents and others have displayed remarkable courage and dedication throughout the operation. But the greatest heroism of all was that of the Falashas themselves. To understand something of the Falashas and why they were waiting to be taken 'on wings of eagles' to Israel in 1984, it will be necessary to go back to the origins of this remarkable tribe and to trace their complex and exciting history within the lands of the Amhara emperors.

CHAPTER TWO

Beta Israel:
A Warrior Race

The Falashas, the Jews of Ethiopia, like the Bene Israel of western India or the Jews of Kai Feng Fu in China, have long inhabited the border regions of the Jewish world. An Agau people, their hundreds of scattered villages are at heights of 6–7,000 feet in the beautiful mountains north of Lake Tana, the source of the Blue Nile, and towards the towering Semien range in the north-eastern part of what is today Gondar province. The nearest town is Gondar, which, until Addis Ababa was built in 1887, was the major city in Ethiopia. Other smaller groups live in the provinces of Wollo and Tigre. They inhabit remote and inaccessible areas and, until recent times, had no contacts with the outside world. Although Jews living in Ethiopia were mentioned in Greek sources as long ago as the second century BC, the first hint we have of the existence of a fully fledged, independent Jewish community in Ethiopia is to be found in an extraordinary work, the *Book of Eldad*, written in the ninth century by a Jewish traveller, Eldad ha-Dani. But fact and fiction are mingled in such uncertain quantities in this work that Eldad, who himself claimed to be of the lost tribe of Dan and has been thought by some to be a Falasha, can scarcely be relied upon. Benjamin of Tudela, the great Jewish traveller of the twelfth century, made brief mention of Ethiopian Jews in his account of a journey he undertook from the Yemen to Egypt.

Mountainous Ethiopia in general was cut off from the rest of the world. In Gibbon's *Decline and Fall of the Roman Empire*, he wrote: 'Encompassed on all sides by the enemies of their religion, the Ethiopians slept nearly one thousand years, forgetful of the world by whom they were forgotten.' With the

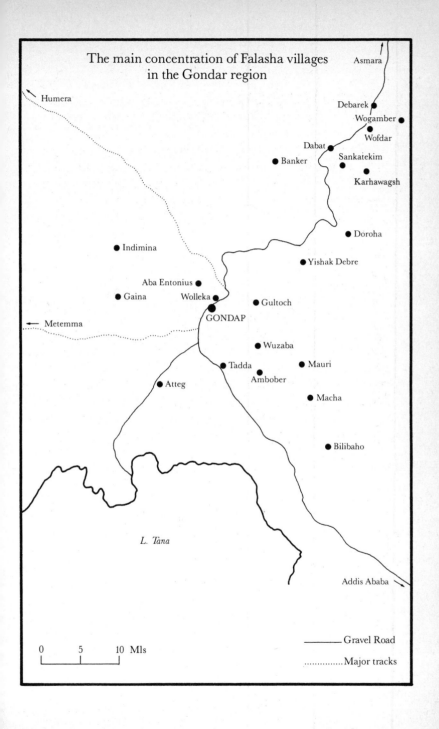

The main concentration of Falasha villages
in the Gondar region

Humera

Asmara

Debarek
Wogamber
Wofdar
Dabat
Sankatekim
Banker
Karhawagsh

Doroha

Indimina
Yishak Debre

Aba Entonius
Gaina
Wolleka
Gultoch
GONDAP

Metemma
Wuzaba
Tadda
Mauri
Atteg
Ambober
Macha

Bilibaho

L. Tana

Addis Ababa

0   5   10 Mls

—————— Gravel Road
.... Major tracks

exception of some sixteenth-century Portuguese records, it was not until the publication in 1790 of *Travels to Discover the Source of the Nile* by the Scottish explorer, James Bruce, the Laird of Kinnaird, that any reliable information about the Falashas reached Europe and the Jewish Diaspora.

One of the chief sources for the early history of the Falashas is the body of Christian Ethiopian chronicles written in Ge'ez, the ancient language of Ethiopia, including the national epic, the *Kebra Negast*. The first reference to the Falashas in these Ethiopian annals dates from the middle of the fourteenth century.

After the rise of Christianity in Ethiopia in the fourth century AD, it is believed that those Ethiopians who had accepted Judaism and refused to embrace Christianity were persecuted and in consequence withdrew from the coastal areas to establish their community in the Gondar region, which has remained their home until today. Bruce recorded that the Falashas took 'possession of the rugged, and almost inaccessible rocks, in that high ridge called the Mountains of Samen. One of these, which nature seems to have formed for a fortress, they chose for their metropolis, and it was ever after called the Jews' Rock.' They were reinforced by Jews who were brought as captives from South Arabia, which by now was highly Judaized, by Kaleb, the *negus* (king) of Ethiopia, after his successful campaign of 525 against the king of Himyar. This group settled in the Semien mountains. For the next thousand years the Falashas resisted assimilation as they defended their autonomy against a succession of Ethiopian emperors. Their stubborn and single-minded refusal to submit to Christianity must be seen as one of the proudest chapters in the history of persecuted minorities.

In the tenth century the Falashas, along with other Agau tribes, rose against the ancient Ethiopian dynasty of Axum. Ethiopian tradition has it that they were led by a Jewish queen, Judith, who overthrew the *negus* and went on a wild rampage throughout Ethiopia, destroying churches and pillaging monasteries. According to Bruce, Judith decided 'to establish her religion by the extirpation of the race of Solomon'. This may be pure legend, but it is a legend with wide currency in Ethiopia and it has some bearing on the subsequent history of the Falashas. Emperor Haile Selassie in his autobiography spoke of 'the extermination of Christians when Yodit of the Falasha tribe reigned'. After an attack on a Falasha village in Wollo in 1972, during which around thirty Falashas were killed, the murderers claimed that they were taking revenge on the descendants of the Jewish queen, 'the whore of Axum', who had almost destroyed Ethiopian Christianity nearly a thousand years before.

Between 1137 and 1270 the Zagwe dynasty, of Agau stock, ruled Ethiopia. This line of kings has been resented by Ethiopian tradition on the grounds that they were not of the Solomonic line and therefore not 'Israelites' as the Amhara emperors claimed to be, for the Amhara Christians, unhistorically, trace their lineage back to the union of Solomon and Sheba. The Zagwe kings seem to have left their Falasha Agau cousins in peace. But in 1270 one of the descendants of the ancient Amhara line of Axum, *Negus* Yekuno Amlak, who claimed direct descent from Solomon and Sheba, was restored to the throne. He determined to destroy the power of the Falashas, perhaps because they could not be relied upon in the critical wars against the Muslim kingdoms of the south which for hundreds of years were to threaten the existence of Christianity in the Horn of Africa. Thus began 400 years of war and bloodshed.

For a period the Falashas held the balance of power between the Christians and the Muslims. During the reign of Amda Seyon (1314-44), the Falasha ruler Gideon decided to join forces with the Muslims against their ancestral Christian enemies. But when the Muslim forces laid waste the Falasha territories north of Lake Tana, Gideon changed allegiance; together, the Christian and Falasha armies were able to halt the Muslim invasion. Amda Seyon's gratitude was not long-lasting and, within a short while, his forces were instructed to bring the Falashas to heel and to convert them to the religion of Christ. Under the emperors Dawit and Yeshaq, the Falashas lost even more ground. A decree issued by Yeshaq (1413-

29) declared that 'He who is baptized in the Christian religion may inherit the land of his father. Otherwise let him be a Falasha!' At Kosage, north of Gondar, the Falashas were defeated in what proved to be a decisive battle. Internal Falasha divisions were exploited by the Amharas and by the middle of the fifteenth century the Falashas, now without a king, were only semi-autonomous. Towards the end of the fifteenth century, Judaism in some form started attracting tribes in the Gondar region and thus the Falashas, who were no longer a military threat, became a religious threat to the Amhara rulers. *Negus* Zara Yakob (1434–68), known in the Ethiopian chronicles as 'the exterminator of the Jews', did much to undermine the Falashas. In his work the *Book of Light*, he echoed medieval European belief (of which he might have been aware) by accusing the Jews of eating children. Under Zara Yakob and his successor, Baeda Mariam (1468–78), there were further massacres of the Falashas and many were forced to convert or, like the Marranos of Spain, to profess Christ in public while secretly clinging to their Jewish faith. But there were still some pockets of Falasha resistance in the Semien mountains.

Again the balance of power shifted and in the reign of Lebna Dengel (1508–40) the Falasha leader Gideon and his 'queen', Judith, in an attempt to reassert their independence, joined forces first with the *negus* and then with the Muslim leader Ahmad ibn Ibrahim. The devastation that followed the Muslim conquest had grievous consequences for Ethiopian culture in general. It is quite possible that the lost literary monuments of the Falashas, which were frequently described by them in subsequent centuries, were in fact destroyed during this period when so much of the wider Ethiopian culture was lost. Led by 'Radaet the Jew', the Falashas had some temporary successes against *Negus* Minas and were able to expand their territory. But by the 1580s, the dogged campaign waged by the new *negus*, Sarsa Dengel, forced them back into the most remote areas of the Semien mountains, where they made a last stand. The Amharas had great numerical superiority and one advantage besides: the Falashas were still armed with shields and spears, but by now the Amharas had managed to acquire guns which were destined to change the balance of power in the area. When Sarsa Dengel had cannons brought up into the mountains, the Falashas' fate was sealed. But they fought to the last, and the Christian Ethiopian chronicles made special mention of their incredible valour. Some women preferred to throw themselves to their death from 'the Jews' Rock' than to live a life of captivity. Radaet the Jew was taken and promised his life if he would pay homage to the Virgin Mary. He replied: 'It is forbidden to utter the name of Mary! Hurry! If I am to die, I depart from a world of lies to a world of justice, from darkness to light. Kill me!'

But still the spirit of the Falashas was not quite broken. During the reign of *Negus* Susenyos (1607–23), the oppressed Agau tribes rose in revolt, joined by the Falashas led by an-other Gideon. As Bruce relates it:

The constant success of the king, and the bloody manner in which he pursued his victory, began to alarm Gideon, lest the end should be the extirpation of his whole nation ... the King gave orders to extirpate all the Falasha that were in Foggora, Janfakara, and Bagenarwe, to the borders of Samen: also all that were in Bagla, and in all the districts under their command, wherever they could find them.

The allies of the Falashas were defeated early in the campaign and they were left to bear the onslaught alone. The remaining Falasha strongholds and fortresses were destroyed and much of the population was killed. Those that were spared were promised that if they laid down their arms they could return to their villages. But the promise was soon broken and the remnant were offered the choice faced so often by Jews through the centuries: conversion to Christianity or death. As Bruce wrote: 'Many of them were baptized accordingly and they were all ordered to plow and harrow on the Sabbath day.' But like the Jewish martyrs of the Inquisition many refused to convert and in 1616, during the slaughter that ensued, their leader Gideon was killed. Those that remained were sold into slavery. This last battle marks the end of Falasha autonomy in any real form, although Western travellers wrote of 'Jewish kings' in Ethiopia until the end of the eighteenth century.

Falasha land was confiscated and thereafter Jews had to lease their land from Amhara landowners. For a while they were forbidden upon pain of death to practise their religion, but eventually the ban was dropped. The wars, the bloodshed and the glory were over, but persecution in various forms continued.

At the end of the eighteenth century James Bruce was told that early in the seventeenth century the Falashas could muster 100,000 fighting men. This suggests a total population of at least half a million people, which, considering the trouble the Falashas had given the Amhara emperors for centuries, seems plausible enough. By the middle of the nineteenth century the Falashas were estimated to number between 150,000 and 200,000. Partly as a result of the efforts of Protestant missionaries, by the turn of this century there were less than 50,000. Today there are no more than 28,000 Falashas, only 8,000 of whom are still in Ethiopia. Whatever their importance in medieval Ethiopia might have been, most Ethiopians outside Addis Ababa and the Gondar region have never heard of the Falashas. They are one tiny section of the forty million Christians, Muslims and pagans who make up the second largest black population in Africa.

The living conditions of the Falashas, like those of their Christian neighbours, have changed very little over the years. They inhabit relatively small villages, which are sited near streams or rivers vital for their ritual ablutions. Some villages are exclusively Falasha. Others are mixed, although the Christians and Falashas live in distinct quarters. Their *tukuls* are made of bamboo, straw and mud and are about five metres in diameter. They have a single entrance and bamboo sleeping benches are formed around the walls. Today some Falasha villages boast concrete-built school houses and synagogues. Like other Ethiopians, the Falashas are tall, handsome people. They wear the undyed, loosely woven cotton cloak called the *shamma*, although in recent years some of the younger Falashas in the villages close to Gondar have started wearing Western-style dress. They walk barefoot. Their staple food is the flat porous bread (*injera*) made from a local grain called *teff*. This is dipped into *wat* – a strongly spiced vegetable or meat sauce. Even now, the very remote villages contain no article of modern manufacture except for firearms and the occasional tin bucket. The ox pulls a wooden plough carved by the village carpenter and the sickles and other tools are hand-beaten by a Falasha smith.

The villages consist of apparently random clusters of houses. Their traditional synagogues are much like the domestic huts but a little larger; they are in most respects identical to the village churches. These days the synagogue roof is usually adorned by the six-sided star of David. One of the special features of the Falasha village is the hut (called the house of the curse) reserved for women during the days of menstruation. Here the women follow the injunctions laid down in the book of Leviticus against contact with the rest of the community and spend their days of menstrual confinement busying themselves with their local crafts.

The traditional definition of Ethiopian nationality did not in the past permit the Falashas to play a role in state or regional affairs or to hold public office. There is a proverb which was told to me by a Falasha now living in Jerusalem: 'The sky has no pillar and the Falasha has no land.' For until the 1974 revolution, the Falashas were not permitted under any circumstances to own land. They were, however, able to rent land and they eked out a precarious existence growing *teff* in the fields and raising sheep and hump-backed cattle on the dry grassland dotted with eucalyptus and acacia trees beyond the confines of the village. But because of the restrictions on land ownership the Falashas developed other occupations. Over the centuries they became the artisan class of their part of Ethiopia, specializing in metalwork, pottery, weaving and the building trades. This did nothing for their standing in the community for such work was despised by the Amhara farmers. None the less, in the past they were responsible for some of the finest buildings in Ethiopia and, in Bruce's day, 'carried the art of pottery to a degree of perfection scarcely to be imagined'. To the present day Falasha men have continued to work as craftsmen while their women have looked after the children and engaged in spinning, weaving and pottery. The ceramic figurines, such as Solomon and Sheba embracing each other in bed, which are made in Wolleka, sell well in local markets.

Through their occupation as blacksmiths the Falashas long ago acquired a reputation as being possessed by *buda*, supernatural powers associated with sorcerers and bearers of the evil eye. They were believed by their Amhara neighbours to have the power to turn into hyenas and in this guise to prey upon Christian children. One seventeenth-century traveller reported that Ethiopian Christians considered the Falashas 'the sort of mortals that spit fire and were bred up in hell'. The crucifixion of Christ was attributed to *buda*; it was craftsmen after all who performed the deed: they fashioned the cross and the nails and hammered them through Christ's hands and feet.

In the first half of the nineteenth century Protestant missionaries, ablaze with the idea of converting Jewish souls in every corner of the globe and thereby bringing closer the return of the Messiah and his 1,000-year reign, discovered the remote Falashas. The London Society for the Conversion of the Jews had no lack of support in high places. Lord Shaftesbury, the father-in-law of Lord Palmerston, was one of its most devoted patrons. No expense or effort was spared. As a result of these misguided efforts many thousands of Falashas were converted to Christianity. Matters were not improved by *Negus* Theodore, who, shortly after his coronation in 1855, ordered the conversion of the Falashas as well as other non-Christian sects. His attempts were not so successful as those of the Western missionaries.

Seeing the missionaries succeed where a thousand years of Amhara oppression had failed, despair seized the community. In 1862 many Falashas, seeing no other solution, began to trek to Jerusalem. This was partly out of fear of the missionaries and partly because they thought the Messiah had come (there was some confusion in their minds between the Messiah, whom they called Theodore, and the Emperor Theodore). In full expectation of some miraculous delivery they left their mountain homes totally unprepared for a migration to the Holy Land. They got no further than the neighbouring province of Tigre, where many of them died. In the same year a Falasha called Abba Sagga wrote a letter in Ge'ez to the 'Chief Priest of the Jews in Jerusalem' asking if the time had yet come for the Jews of Ethiopia to return to the promised land:

Has the time arrived that we should return to you, our city, the holy city of Jerusalem? For we are a poor people and have neither prince nor prophet and if the time has arrived send us a letter which will reach us.... They say that the time has arrived; the men of our country say: 'separate yourselves from the Christians and go to your country, Jerusalem, and reunite yourselves with your brothers.'

Abba Sagga received no reply to his letter. The Falashas were to wait 122 years before the time was considered right.

CHAPTER THREE

Are the Falashas Jews?

The question of how Jewish the Falashas are or whether they should properly be regarded as Jews at all is still a burning topic in Israel. Although Operation Moses has provided adequate proof that the State of Israel regards them as Jews, the continuing insistence on the part of the Israeli rabbinate that the Falashas go through some form of symbolic 'renewal of the covenant' indicates that in orthodox circles all doubts have not been laid to rest. Some of the Hasidic and other extreme orthodox groups in Israel and the United States still refuse to recognize the Falashas as Jews in any sense.

But the majority of Jews throughout the world and in Israel now believe that the Falashas are Jews, and if there are problems in such an identification they are prepared to ignore them. Bemused tolerance characterizes the attitude of even those Jews who know that the question is a complex one. Former Prime Minister Menachem Begin, when asked if the Falashas were really Sephardi Jews, replied: 'You ask me if they are Sephardi? I do not know. But one thing I do know, they are not Ashkenazi!'

The Falashas themselves like to maintain that they are descended from the Jews who came to Ethiopia with King Menelik I, who is thought by Ethiopians to be the son of King Solomon and the Queen of Sheba. Indeed, there are a number of theories connecting the Falashas with the Israelites of old. Some claim that when the Hebrews left Egypt at the time of the Exodus a group broke off from the rest and found their way to Ethiopia, where they eventually established their own kingdom. But the most popular and most persistent such theory is that the Falashas are one of the lost tribes of Israel.

After the death of King Solomon a schism came about and ten of the twelve tribes seceded and, under Jeroboam, formed the Northern Kingdom. When the Northern Kingdom fell 200 years later, the majority of the Israelites were forcibly deported to Assyria, where they soon lost their separate identity and assimilated. But the Jews never entirely accepted the loss of the ten tribes. Jeremiah and Ezekiel both prophesied their eventual return and later Jewish literature made frequent mention of their continued existence, particularly in the fabled land of Sambation.

Many orthodox Jews, including former Chief Rabbi, Ovadia Yosef, believe that the Falashas are the lost tribe of Dan. Unfortunately, this romantic notion has no historical substance. Indeed, there is no evidence to support the view that the Falashas are descended from Israelite stock at all. However, the legend of the ten tribes has world-wide appeal, and it is not surprising that the international media seized upon this aspect of Operation Moses with headlines such as 'Rescue of the Lost Tribe'. In fact, the origins of the Falashas, to the extent that they can be determined, are no less romantic than the myths which have been enlisted to explain them. But they are to be found not in the Land of Israel but in Ethiopia itself.

The Falashas, as Edward Ullendorff has written, are 'Ethiopians of Agaw stock who practise a peculiar kind of Judaism'. In scholarly circles no one would dissent from this view. The real question is not where did the Falashas come from, but where did their 'peculiar Judaism' come from?

The ancient Ethiopian Kingdom of Axum was founded in the first century AD. Until the conversion to Christianity of its greatest king, Ezana, 400 years later, the culture of Axum had been greatly influenced by the Semitic and Judaic concepts which had taken root in South Arabia. There was continuous two-way traffic between South Arabia and Ethiopia, which are separated only by the narrow straits of Bab el Mandeb. It can be assumed that the Falashas are the descendants of those Judaized and Semitized elements within the Axumite Kingdom which rejected Christianity. Included among these may have been Jews, Arabians or Ethiopians who had converted to Judaism and Ethiopians who had been reluctant to exchange their broadly Judaic beliefs for Christian ones. It should be remembered that at the beginning of the Christian era, Judaism, in one form or another, had millions of adherents mainly around the Mediterranean, only a minority of whom were from Palestine. There were certainly Jewish converts in South Arabia as well as Palestinian Jews who had migrated there before the destruction of Jerusalem by Titus in AD 70. The name Falasha, which means 'émigré', perhaps originally referred to Arabian Jews or Arabian converts to Judaism who had left Arabia and settled in Ethiopia. It can be presumed that this migration of people or ideas took place before the third century AD when the Jewish Oral Law was codified, because there are no elements in the Falasha religion which reflect any awareness of post-canonical rabbinic Judaism. If there was any admixture of Jewish blood 2,000 years ago, there is certainly no sign of it today. The Falashas are indistinguishable, physically, from any other Ethiopians of their region.

Wolf Leslau, one of the more reliable writers on the Falashas, has accepted, with some reservations, that the religion practised by the Falashas is Judaism and that they are therefore Jews. But it is a Judaism which is very different from that which is practised elsewhere. This is not least because, until the nineteenth century, the Falashas were completely isolated from the Jewish world. Indeed, they believed that they were the only Jews left. Unlike most other Jews, the Falashas have no knowledge of Hebrew – their sacred texts are written in Ge'ez (a language which only the priests understand), as are the scriptures of the Ethiopian Christians. Under the probable influence of Christian Ethiopia they have adopted a monastic tradition which is extremely unusual, although not entirely unheard of, in Judaism. But the chief peculiarity of the religion of the Falashas is that they have no knowledge of rabbinic Judaism, its texts, its refinements of biblical law (such as the regulations prohibiting the mixing of meat and milk based on the biblical 'thou shalt not seethe the kid in its mother's milk'), its calendar or its post-Exilic feasts (such as Purim or

Hanukkah). What they do practise however is, in many essen-tial ways, Old Testament pre-Exilic Judaism, based on a lit-eral obedience to the Pentateuch. Their central belief is in the 'God of Israel, the Invisible, Creator of Heaven and Earth'. They adhere strictly to biblical laws concerning the Sabbath, circumcision, the animals, birds and fish permitted for food, contact with the dead and the laws of ritual uncleanness, especially for women after childbirth and during menstrua-tion. In line with biblical practice, the organization and cele-bration of prayer and religious ritual among the Falashas is in the hands of a priest, *Kahen* (Hebrew *Kohen*), whose functions differ markedly from those of a rabbi whose responsibilities are the maintenance of religious standards and specifically the study and exposition of the sacred texts. The Falashas still practise animal sacrifice, seasoning the beast with salt as the Book of Leviticus enjoins. The animal is slaughtered by the priest, who uses a special two-edged knife reserved for this purpose. For Jews elsewhere, of course, sacrifice ceased with the destruction of the Second Temple, when prayer became a substitute for sacrifice.

Many of these elements are to be found in Ethiopian Chris-tianity, which is intensely conservative and highly Judaized. But the Falashas have their own specific customs and beliefs which set their religion apart from Ethiopian Christianity, the most important of which is their complete rejection of Jesus and their belief in the coming (not the return) of the Messiah.

The Falashas have maintained a strong spiritual attach-ment to the Land of Israel throughout their history. Whenever a Falasha prayed, he would first turn in the direction of Jerusalem, and Falasha literature and prayers deal constantly with such themes as the 'return' to Zion and the re-establish-ment of priestly worship in the temple. Their love of Zion is no different, in essence, to that of any other Jewish group throughout the Diaspora.

Despite the obvious differences, the Falashas' elaboration of the ancient faith of Israel is in some ways comparable to the development of post-Exilic Judaism. Much of the point of rabbinic Judaism is to set the Jewish people apart from other nations, to maintain their ancient traditions and to prevent assimilation with the host societies among which they lived. This was done by the creation of an immensely intricate system of laws, which govern every aspect of a Jew's life. The Falashas, for their part, defended themselves against assimilation by laying particular stress on matters of ritual cleanliness. Until very recently, when a Falasha happened to touch a non-Falasha he was considered impure until he had bathed himself. Such emphatic observance clearly helped isolate the Falashas from Christian society in the same way that the Jewish dietary regulations and the prohibitions against drinking wine with non-Jews helped to keep Jewish society apart elsewhere.

Throughout the ages the Falashas managed to maintain a quite separate identity from their Christian neighbours. In *The Blue Nile* Alan Moorehead wrote: 'The Ethiopians were eaters of raw meat, heavy drinkers, uncouth in their manners and given to wild and primitive passions ... the Ethiopians on their icy heights huddled together with their cattle at night and seldom washed.' The Falashas, on the other hand, cooked their meat, were sober by inclination and were so relentlessly hygienic that the Amhara accused them of smelling of water. Standards of sexual propriety were equally stringent among the Falashas. If a girl was discovered on her wedding night not to be a virgin, she was expelled from the 'House of Israel' and ceased to be a Falasha. Intermarriage with non-Falashas was unknown.

Whether the Falashas are descendants of converts to Judaism or whether they are a fossilized remnant of Judaizing tendencies within Ethiopia two millennia ago is unclear. They are probably the product of both developments. What is clear, however, is that they abide by Abraham's covenant and have kept faith with the essentials of the ancient religion of Israel. They have done this despite the blandishments of Western missionaries and, most recently, religious oppression by the Marxist government of Ethiopia.

The fact that the Falashas are not 'ethnically Jewish' has no great significance. European Jewry's ethnic origins owe a great deal to early converts to Judaism and to the admixture of the Khazars from central Asia, who adopted Judaism in the ninth century. Indeed, the ethnic composition of Jews throughout the Diaspora has been so complicated by the vicissitudes of exile that it is a nonsense to speak of a Jewish 'race' at all. A Falasha was once asked what *he* thought the ethnic relationship of Falashas to other Jews was. He outlined the history of his people and answered the question by asking another: 'Was Abraham, our father, white or black?'

To most external observers the fact that the Falashas have faithfully upheld a form of Judaism for centuries despite constant oppression and persecution is proof enough that they are Jews and that they should be considered as such. But for Jewish orthodoxy the matter is not so simple and it was some time before the rabbinate was able to make up its mind on the issue.

The Jewish world was unaware of the existence of the Falashas until the end of the eighteenth century. When Bruce's *Travels to Discover the Source of the Nile* brought news of the Falashas to the Jews of Europe, they did not respond with any great urgency. There were many exotic Jewish communities throughout the world of whom little was known: the Tats of Dagestan and Azerbaijan, the Cochin Jews of Kerala, the Krimchaks of Crimea. The Falashas were perhaps just one more. It was not until reports of Protestant activity among the Falashas started reaching European Jews in the mid-nineteenth century that Jewish organizations, justifiably indignant, started to take an interest in saving their co-religionists, if such they were, from the clutches of the missionaries. The newly formed *Alliance Israélite Universelle* sent Joseph Halévy, a French Semitics scholar of some note, to report back on the situation of the Falashas and to ascertain whether they were indeed Jews. His reports confirmed that they were Jews and that the Western missions were sparing no effort or expense to convert them to Christianity. Thousands had been persuaded that it was only their woeful backwardness and ignorance that had prevented them from realizing that the Messiah, for whom they had waited so long, had in fact come some 2,000 years before. But Halévy's words fell on unsympathetic ears and his report was shelved.

The Falashas were effectively ignored by world Jewry for the next fifty years. But in 1904, Jacques Faitlovich, the greatest champion of the Falashas, made the first of many visits to their communities. One of the results of his visit was that a number of pro-Falasha committees were set up in Europe and America, the purpose of which was to establish links between the Falashas and Jews elsewhere. Faitlovich maintained close contacts with the Falashas through the inter-war years and beyond. The initiative which was to have the greatest long-term influence on the community was the encouragement and financial assistance Faitlovich gave to a handful of young Falashas to study in Europe. These students were to provide future leaders who were aware not only of the outside Jewish world, and a great deal besides, but also of the Zionist movement and its aspirations. Upon their return, these young men were much admired and looked up to by the Falasha villagers as a result of their exposure to Western ways and the education which they had received abroad. Subsequently, they were to play an important part in the creation of new Falasha perceptions of the world: there were Jews elsewhere and they, the Falashas, were their brothers.

In 1921, the enormously respected Ashkenazi Chief Rabbi of Palestine, Avraham Kook, appealed to world Jewry to 'save our Falasha brethren from extinction and to rescue 50,000 souls of the House of Israel from oblivion. A holy obligation rests upon our entire nation to improve the lot of the Falashas in Ethiopia and to bring their young children to Jewish centres in Palestine and the Diaspora.' This passionate and no doubt heartfelt appeal had little impact on Jewish thinking because for the next thirty years history intervened. The birthpangs of the Jewish National Home in Palestine and the almost complete annihilation of European Jewry during the Second World War kept the focus of attention elsewhere. After the War of Independence in 1948, Israel was flooded by waves of immigration. One hundred thousand survivors of the Nazi death camps were gradually brought into the country. They were followed by the Jews of Morocco and those of Yemen who were flown to Israel in the dramatic and much publicized airlift known as Operation Magic Carpet. In Operation Ezra and Nehemiah, 120,000 Jews were flown in from hostile Iraq. The state was stretched to its limits and the Falashas were forgotten.

In the 1950s the infant State of Israel, needful of friends in a largely hostile world, started making overtures of friendship to Africa. The ill-fated Africa policy that was to develop was thought by some to be complicated by the existence of black African 'Jews' and the problems of the Falashas were ignored. Ben-Gurion, founding father of the Jewish state, and several of his ministers listened with attention to accounts of the Falashas brought back by Jewish travellers. Ben-Gurion held the view that a Jew is someone who believes himself to be a Jew and he was in favour of Falasha immigration. His advisers, however, were not. Emperor Haile Selassie, the Conquering Lion of the Tribe of Judah, the Elect of God, was an occasional friend of Israel but was opposed to Falasha emigration on the grounds that it might encourage other tribal minorities to demand autonomy or special treatment. In addition, no matter what Rabbi Kook had argued thirty years before, there were now a number of scholars of international standing who insisted that the Falashas were not Jews at all.

During the 1950s and 1960s, the argument that the Falashas were not Jews was prevalent in Israel. It was admitted that they respected the Sabbath and maintained some of the *kashrut* regulations; but they were illiterate African tribesmen whose priests did not even know a word of Hebrew or anything at all of rabbinic Judaism. Even their supposedly Jewish traits were shared by Christian Ethiopians and by certain non-Christian groups such as the Qemant, while even the Emperor regarded himself as a direct descendant of Solomon and Sheba and thought of himself as an 'Israelite'. These were some of the arguments advanced by Israeli and Jewish spokesmen and they are not without historical foundation. But the stand taken by the rabbinate and the Israeli government was not universally admired and increasingly vocal opposition to it began to emerge within Israel and throughout the Diaspora, particularly in the United States. Many Jews throughout the world thought that the Falashas were Jews. One was Jacques Faitlovich, now an old man. Almost single-handedly he managed to persuade the Jewish Agency, the institution of the World Zionist Organization responsible for immigration to Israel, to take some interest in the Falashas. In 1954 the Agency set up a teacher-training establishment for them in Asmara, which was to serve as the first link between the Falashas and the Jewish state. A year later a group of Falasha children were sent to study in Ra'anana in Israel. Many of them subsequently returned to Ethiopia to teach. But in 1955 Faitlovich died. Two years later the Agency school in Asmara was closed down and again the Falashas were left to their own devices.

Over the next few years reports reached Israel and the West of local persecution of the Falashas and, in 1960, an open letter was sent by the Falashas to Jewish organizations in Israel, Europe and America asking for help. Over the next decade a number of individuals and organizations made great efforts to assist them, particularly in the area of education. In 1969 the American Pro-Falasha Committee, founded years before by Faitlovich, was reactivated and gradually Western support grew. But the initiatives were on a minuscule scale. Many of those Jews in the West who were concerned with the Falashas believed that the real solution to their plight lay in emigration to Israel. But as the government of Israel did not recognize the Falashas as Jews it would not allow them to enter the country under the Law of Return, which gives every Jew the right to full Israeli citizenship. In addition, the *negusa negast*, Haile Selassie, would not allow them to leave Ethiopia.

Whether they were officially regarded as Jews or not, Falashas trickled into Israel. The run from the Ethiopian port Massawa to Eilat was just over forty-eight hours. Some Falashas got jobs on Greek freighters and jumped ship in Eilat; others managed to save the money for an air ticket from El Al, the Israeli airline, which in 1970 established a regular service from Addis Ababa to Lod. But the Israelis did not make it easy. One woman whose son had made his way to Israel applied to the Israeli embassy in Addis Ababa for a visa, explaining that she wished to join him. She was told that she could not visit the country unless she had $600 in travellers' cheques. Three weeks later she returned to the embassy with a cross hung around her neck and explained to another official that she was a Christian wanting to go on pilgrimage to Israel. She was given a visa on the spot. Israeli officials now acknowledge that for some years there was a policy of active discouragement of Falasha immigration. A former speaker of the Knesset, Yisrael Yeshayahu, advised the Falashas to solve their problems by converting to Christianity.

Meanwhile, the small band of Falashas who managed to make their way to Israel formed themselves into the Israel Falasha Committee. It was led by Professor Tartakower, a sociologist and demographer whose academic life had started in his native Poland, and an Ethiopian Jew of Yemenite extraction by the name of Ovadia Hazzi, who had become the Israeli army's senior sergeant-major. The society headed by this strangely matched pair played a major part in persuading the religious authorities that the Falashas were indeed Jews.

In 1973, the Sephardi Chief Rabbi of Israel, Ovadia Yosef, basing himself on earlier rabbinic rulings, most notably by the sixteenth-century Chief Rabbi of Egypt, David ben Solomon Ibn Avi Zimrah (or the Radbaz as he is known for short), and invoking the views of former Chief Rabbi Kook, declared that the Falashas were 'Jews who must be saved from absorption and assimilation. We are obligated to speed up their immigration into Israel ... for whoever saves a single soul in Israel, it is as though he had saved the whole world.'

The rabbi's ruling was given an enthusiastic response by the few Falashas who had somehow found their way to Israel. Zechariah Yonah, a leader of the 150-strong community, greeted the 'wonderful decision' and said, 'We have been waiting years for this.' A Falasha nurse, Ora Mekouria, simply said: 'This is our place.'

Ovadia Yosef's decision inspired a wave of support for the

Falashas throughout the Jewish world. Articles started appearing in the Jewish press and pressure on Israel to do something for the Ethiopian Jews began to mount. In 1974 the old American Pro-Falasha Committee, started by Faitlovich, and a newer organization, The Friends of Beta Israel Community in Ethiopia, founded by Dr Graenum Berger, merged to form the American Association for Ethiopian Jews (AAEJ). The new organization was headed by Berger, whose passionate concern for the Falashas was to bring him into conflict with the Israeli authorities frequently over the next decade. Berger is a tough, feisty man with decided views and a strong anti-authoritarian bias. Since his first encounter with the Falashas in the 1950s, Berger has been convinced that the only impediment to Falasha emigration to Israel was Israel's reluctance to take them. For the next ten years his organization was to provide a forum for carping criticism of Israeli Falasha policy.

The foundation for Israel's future policy regarding the Falashas was laid in April 1975 when the *Misrad haPenim*, the Israeli Ministry of the Interior, acting on the advice of an inter-ministerial committee, converted the religious ruling of the Sephardi Chief Rabbi into law. Henceforth the Falashas were entitled to enter Israel and receive automatic Israeli citizenship under the 1950 Law of Return.

CHAPTER FOUR

Revolution

In the mountainous region of Gondar, it was believed that if a Jew crossed on to Christian land the grass would never grow again. It was this sort of local prejudice rather than state discrimination which traditionally made life difficult for the Falashas. During the reign of Haile Selassie (1930–74) peasants, whether Christians, Muslims or Jews, were treated with indifference and little that happened in Addis Ababa had any bearing on the life of the impoverished peasantry, particularly in the remote mountain areas. But local factors ensured that the Ethiopian Jews were less well off than their Christian peasant neighbours.

Since the loss of their political autonomy three and a half centuries before, the Falashas had not owned their land. In the Gondar region, they were the only religious group not to own its land. The Christian peasants had to suffer the burden of medievally rapacious land-taxes, but the Falashas had to pay the land-tax in addition to a high rent which was often as much as fifty per cent of an annual crop.

These economic pressures were augmented by social ones. The Falashas were scorned by the Amhara because many of them worked as artisans and feared because they were thought to be the killers of Christ. It was commonly believed in the villages that the Falashas brought Christian corpses back to life to work their fields for them at night. The Falashas were blamed by their neighbours for every misfortune which befell the areas in which they lived. In the mixed villages Falashas were required to apologize for local set-backs to the village leaders and, after the revolution, to the peasant associations.

For a Falasha peasant, farming land that was often adjacent

to Christian land, there were constant difficulties. The Christians in some villages, claiming that the water was theirs, objected to the Falashas using the streams and rivers for their cattle. The Falashas had no rights. They were the untouchables of Ethiopia. When travelling from one village to another the Falashas would often try to pass themselves off as Christians. Various forms of social camouflage were adopted: many Falasha women tattooed a cross on their foreheads, hoping thereby to avoid some of the indignities that were the daily accompaniment of Falasha life.

Haile Selassie's modest attempts at reform had little impact upon the lives of the Falashas. But in 1974 he was deposed and the 2,000-year-old monarchy was abolished. The first act of the revolution was to destroy the power of the landed classes and the church, which owned vast estates throughout the country, by redistributing the land to the peasantry. In the southern provinces the reforms were successful, but in the north they were firmly resisted and fierce internecine warfare broke out. An internal power struggle which culminated in a gun battle among the members of the Dergue, the military council, brought Lieutenant-Colonel Mengistu Haile Mariam to power in February 1977.

The group that resisted the land reforms most fiercely was the counter-revolutionary Ethiopian Democratic Union (EDU), initially supported by some of the ousted royal family. Armed militias commanded by the old nobility and landlords, often operating out of the Sudan, caused devastation in parts of northern Ethiopia. As the landlords saw it, the only way for them to avoid losing their land was to eliminate the people who were in need of it. In the Gondar region the Falashas were one group which traditionally had not owned its land and so stood to gain most from the land reforms. Consequently, the Falashas were made the target of EDU raids and, between 1977 and 1979, hundreds and perhaps thousands of them were forced to flee their remote villages and move to areas of greater Falasha concentration. In one village in Gondar seventy-eight Falashas were killed in an EDU attack. During this period, which came to be known as the 'white terror', hundreds of Jews are thought to have been killed, some were forced into slavery and many more made homeless. Christian villagers also suffered as a result of the unrest and many thousands of them fled over the border into Sudan.

The plight of the Falashas was compounded by the fact that they were also singled out and attacked by units of the extreme left-wing Ethiopian People's Revolutionary Party (EPRP) which, like the EDU, was waging sporadic war against the Dergue. Violently anti-Zionist, the EPRP attacked Falasha villagers because they were Jews and were thought to have Zionist sympathies. Thus the Falashas were harassed for different reasons by rebellious factions from both sides. The government made every effort to crush the forces of the EDU and the EPRP. During the so-called 'red terror', government forces committed random acts of violence throughout Gondar in order to terrorize the local population and warn off the rebel troops. The Falashas were sometimes attacked by the Dergue's forces, chiefly because they were the most vulnerable group and would be able to offer little resistance.

Although the Falashas had not participated in the revolution against the *ancien régime*, they were not initially opposed to it. In one sense they were its greatest beneficiaries since they now had the right to own land. But until the end of the 1970s they were not often able to exercise this right. Sometimes the EDU or the EPRP forced them from their land. Sometimes local officials were reluctant to implement central policy. Bayuhe Melku, a Falasha who left Ethiopia for Israel in 1980, said: 'When the revolution came they promised punishment for the anti-Semites and we were given land. But the old landlords kept on coming to take what we had grown, as they always had before.' Unwilling to lose their ancient privileges, the landlords were often able to harness local prejudice against the Falashas and incite their Christian peasant neighbours against them.

By 1980, Major Melaku, the young governor of Gondar province and a veteran of the palace coup which had brought Mengistu to power, had seen the forces of the EDU and the EPRP defeated. In the relatively stable months that followed, efforts were made to implement the provisions of the land reforms which thus far had only brought suffering to the Jews. Gradually, land to the extent of about twenty-five acres a family was given to the Falashas, except those in the more remote villages. Often, however, the reallocation of land was in the hands of peasant associations, who were not entirely in sympathy with the egalitarian views of the revolution and saw nothing wrong with insisting that the despised Falashas should be allotted the inferior land that they had always farmed.

The Marxist regime went to considerable lengths to aid the various minorities throughout Ethiopia during the early years of the revolution. Ethiopian Jews, like other minorities, were invited to participate fully in the revolution. In regional and youth associations Falashas who adopted the correct ideological stance were accepted on their own merits. One Falasha reached the rank of sub-district chief administrator and many others achieved fairly important office. This policy was in accordance with paragraph 5 of the programme of the National Democratic Revolution of Ethiopia, which states: 'No nationality will dominate another since the history, culture, language and religion of each nationality will have equal recognition, in accordance with the spirit of socialism.'

In time, however, this early emphasis was to change. Indeed, the central government eventually conceived that the only way to govern effectively the myriad cultures which go to make up Ethiopia was to impose uniformity from above.

The revolutionary slogan 'Ethiopia Tikdem' or 'Ethiopia First' began to imply the eradication of minority and tribal cultures as a national priority. Amharic was given pre-eminence in all areas and it was officially hoped that in time it would succeed in replacing all the local languages. At the same time, although the Marxist government was anti-religious as a matter of course and had as its ultimate purpose the eradication of religion from Ethiopian society, Christian Amhara culture was seen as the model for assimilation. It is clear that the real power of the church in Ethiopia had been destroyed when it had lost its estates during the land reform programme. Subsequently, many important church leaders 'disappeared'. But grass-roots support for the church was too important a factor to be ignored with impunity. Cautiously the Dergue declared Coptic Christianity and Islam to be the only two officially recognized religions of Ethiopia. This meant that in the years to come the minority religions had to bear the brunt of the anti-religious measures of the government.

Classified as 'foreign religions', Roman Catholics, Methodists, Pentecostalists, Seventh Day Adventists and Jews came under increasing pressure. The Falashas, for the first time in recent history, were now subject to official government discrimination. While Christians and Muslims could worship freely, celebrate their distinctive feasts and bring up their children in their own religious and cultural traditions, the Jews and the other proscribed groups could not. In Gondar province, where the Jews were a fairly significant religious minority, the authorities did everything in their power to force their assimilation into Christian society. The age-old struggle was being waged again. The chief protagonist in the struggle against the Falashas was Major Melaku, who had a deeply felt personal antipathy for them. Exploiting traditional dislike of the Jews, he blamed them for the crop failures in 1980 and for the resulting famine in the north of the province.

The presence in Gondar of the Jewish aid organization ORT (Organization for Rehabilitation and Training) provided something of a check to excessive persecution of the Falashas. To the Gondar authorities ORT was a valuable asset. It provided over a million dollars a year in foreign currency and ran a non-sectarian development programme which benefited the whole province. Among other things ORT had built roads and water-well systems and had distributed farming aids. On the other hand, ORT reinforced the ties the Falashas had with Israel. Unwilling to assimilate, the Falashas now had a choice which they had never had in the past. Because of the 1975 Israeli ruling which gave the Falashas the right to Israeli citizenship, they could go to Israel. But this Melaku was determined to prevent.

From the end of 1977 small groups of Falashas started fleeing into Sudan, where they joined the thousands of Christians who had founded refugee villages on the Sudanese side of the border. As groups reached Israel, the news was transmitted to Gondar and this gave further impetus to the migration. In July 1980 around ninety Jews were arrested near the Sudanese border and sent back to serve prison sentences in Gondar. In an attempt to isolate the 'Zionist agitators', they were all tortured. For revolutionary Ethiopia, 'racist' and 'imperialist' Israel was anathema. For Melaku it was deeply humiliating that his subjects should want to go there and be prepared to risk torture and even death to do so.

For the Jews who were caught trying to escape there was no mercy. Classified as 'political prisoners', they were not entitled to be tried in the normal way but were sentenced by officers of the security service. The prison conditions were unspeakable, the tortures barbaric. A favourite was the 'bastinado': beating the feet for a long period with a stout club. With successive beatings the feet swell and the torture becomes more and more painful. Some Falashas were permanently crippled by the bastinado. In 1983, Ephraim, a boy of fifteen from the Falasha village of Ambober, showed a visitor the scars on his feet.

I was in prison for four months. They turn you upside down, put a fire there and beat you with sticks. I did not do anything. They said I was a spy and wanted to help the *shiftas* [anti-government bandits]. Now what can I do? I cannot walk to school in Gondar and I cannot help my family in the fields.

The Jews were often treated worse than other prisoners. Even sympathizers with the EDU or EPRP were still considered 'good Ethiopians', whereas the Falashas were viewed as traitors and spies who were trying to reach 'racist' Israel.

In July 1981, suspecting perhaps that Jewish employees of ORT were helping to organize the exodus of Falashas, Melaku decided to force ORT to leave the province. He was supported by higher authorities: Fisseha Geda, the national commis-

sioner for tourism in Addis Ababa, accused ORT of smuggling
Falashas out of Ethiopia to Sudan and onward to Israel,
which 'had to be stopped for they are totally Ethiopians'. The
Falashas' most immediate link with the outside world was cut.
The Governor now forbade the practice of the Jewish religion
and the teaching of Hebrew, which had by this time been
taught in Gondar for almost thirty years. Hebrew books were
confiscated. The Ethiopian authorities argued that Hebrew
was only being taught as preparation for emigration to Israel.
One by one the Jewish schools and synagogues were closed.
Students caught talking to tourists were questioned and sometimes imprisoned. Later in 1981, the Falashas were deprived
of contacts with tourists and diplomats. Ethiopian tourist bro-
chures continued to offer visits to the Falasha villages, but
interested foreigners were prevented from making these trips.
At one public burning almost 200 Hebrew books were destroyed. The teachers and priests were arrested, tortured and
harassed. Brehanu, a Jewish priest in Chowda, a village of 500
Falashas in the middle of the Semien mountains, some three
days' trek from Gondar, was imprisoned in 1981 for fifteen
months on accusations of 'spreading black magic' around
neighbouring Christian villages.

The following year the United States State Department
Report on Human Rights Practices stressed that the Ethiopian
government appeared to tolerate discrimination against certain 'ethnic groups' and that the Falashas had been in a worse
position since the middle of 1981 than any other group in the
Gondar province. The report noted that the Christians had
access to their churches whereas, since 1981, the synagogues
and ORT schools had been closed.

In order to halt the exodus of Jews across the border,
Melaku tightened the regulations governing local travel passes.
In the days of Haile Selassie such passes were unknown and
were introduced only in the late 1970s, when large areas of
the province were in the hands of the EDU and the EPRP. The
travel pass had to be signed by the chairman of the local
peasant association before its bearer could start on a journey.
To control travel in such wild and mountainous country was

not easy: Draconian measures were needed. Anyone without a pass could be arrested. Although by 1981 the EDU and the EPRP had been routed, Melaku insisted that the use of the travel pass be continued. The regulations for Falashas were more stringent than for Christians. A Falasha was not allowed to go any further than the next peasant association without special permission in writing from his own association. Christians were allowed to undertake journeys of up to a week without having a pass. A Falasha found without a pass was assumed to be trying to escape and was liable to imprisonment.

Nevertheless the exodus continued. Melaku introduced a policy of punishing the relatives of those who had fled to Sudan. Fathers were ordered to report the disappearance of a son or daughter within twenty-four hours. Any father failing to comply with the regulation was to be imprisoned and tortured.

In early June 1983, having discovered that six Jews had left one village in Gondar, the authorities seized fifteen other Jews, including some relatives of those who had escaped, tortured them and put them in prison. Two weeks later sixty Jews left the same village. The authorities then used different tactics. The Falasha villagers were warned that many of those who had left the villages had died on the way to Sudan, many of the women had been raped and those who had reached Israel had been sold as slaves.

Earlier, a young Falasha had been arrested for being a 'Zionist' agent and for trying to 'escape'. Shortly before his arrest, he wrote a letter to his friend who had managed to reach Israel in the previous year. He wrote:

We will not sell our souls to lose our faith and our traditions. We will repeat the story again and again until maybe only one man will remain to tell it – to ask for help to save a whole nation, a whole tribe, that was dedicated for a thousand years to its faith beyond the mountains of Ethiopia.

The attempts to stamp out Falasha traditions and practices were stepped up, using the 'national service campaigners', the

Zematcha. These were students delegated by the government with the demanding task of bringing literacy and Marxist ideology to the remote peasant villages. The *Zematcha* were instructed to persuade the Falashas to renounce their faith and traditions. The customs of *kashrut* and hygiene were mocked and ridiculed by the young cadres. But the custom which was most obvious and which was most attacked by the *Zematcha*, as it had been by *Negus* Susenyos, was the observance of the Sabbath. It was finally decided by the local government to hold market days on Saturday in an attempt to get the Jews to give up the Sabbath. Although it caused considerable economic hardship, the Falashas refused to relinquish their ancient practice. But these were difficult times. Perfectly aware of their own backwardness, the younger Falashas were not impervious to the taunts of their more educated contemporaries.

Although theoretically the revolution had transformed the status of the Falashas and brought them the greatest benefit of all in a country like Ethiopia – land – a variety of other circumstances as well as old prejudices combined to make their position even more difficult than it had been before. Victims of the 'white' reaction to the revolution, then of the 'red terror', attacked as a proscribed minority whose specific cultural identity had to be destroyed, the Falashas finally decided in growing numbers that their future lay elsewhere.

Towards the end of 1983, seeing that force had succeeded merely in driving them away, the Ethiopian authorities started to soften their policy towards the Falashas. Synagogues and schools were reopened. Jewish tourists were again admitted to certain of the Falasha villages and fewer efforts were made to undermine Falasha culture. As in the Soviet Union, the ban on Hebrew education and Jewish emigration remained in force. The latter, of course, was not a specifically anti-Falasha measure, any more than the military draft which was gradually extended to Falasha areas. No one was allowed to leave Ethiopia.

The improved situation was remarked on by a Canadian B'nai Brith fact-finding mission which visited Ethiopia in

March 1984. Don Jubas, a member of the mission and president of the Canadian B'nai Brith, said that they had found 'no specifically anti-Jewish legislation or discrimination. That is important in view of the wrong information that is being fed to the media. One has to understand the special situation. There are civil wars going on – and that means military draft, not just for the Jews but for everyone.' But for many Falashas the reforms were too late.

CHAPTER FIVE

A New Policy

During Haile Selassie's reign, Israel's relations with Ethiopia had generally been cordial. The Mossad had trained the Emperor's secret police, Israeli industrial and agricultural enterprises were set up in Ethiopia, and scientific and cultural exchanges were encouraged. However, in the wake of the Yom Kippur War relations between the two states were severed and were subsequently not renewed by the new Marxist regime. None the less, even though there were no diplomatic relations between the states, Israel carried on supplying Ethiopia with Israeli arms, spare parts for American-made weapons and military advisers. When Menachem Begin came to power, there were some signs of *rapprochement* between the two states. Begin sent an official communication to Mengistu asking him to apply humanitarian considerations to the issue of the Falashas and to let them emigrate to Israel if they so wished. Mengistu did not reply directly to this request but a little later, after President Sadat's visit to Jerusalem, when Begin was about to visit President Carter in Washington, he received a communication from Mengistu shortly before his departure, asking him for his help in securing American military aid for Ethiopia in its struggle against Soviet-backed Somali forces in the Ogaden. Mengistu also stressed that he would continue to need Israeli arms and American parts from Israel, but it was imperative that supplies of such should remain a closely guarded secret. Begin promised his help on both counts in exchange for Mengistu's co-operation on the Falashas. But in Washington, Jimmy Carter refused to go along with Begin's suggestions. He considered Ethiopia's human rights record appalling and felt that the United States could not support such a regime, however indirectly. Meanwhile, the USSR agreed to arm and train the Ethiopian army. Begin still held his arms card (the Ethiopians particularly needed spares for their American T54 tanks), and for a few months the Ethiopian authorities turned a blind eye to the emigration of Falashas to Israel.

In February 1978, the secret pact between Israel and Ethiopia was uncovered when Foreign Minister Moshe Dayan publicly confirmed at a press conference in Switzerland that Israel had been supplying arms to Ethiopia. Mengistu's Marxist and enthusiastically anti-Zionist regime was put in an awkward position. Arms sales came to a halt (although they were to be renewed later) and the idea of 'legal' emigration of Falashas from Ethiopia had to be abandoned. Authoritative Israeli sources insist that Dayan's leak was deliberate: not because he was opposed to Falasha immigration into Israel, but rather because he was profoundly uneasy about supplying arms to what he considered to be an 'evil regime'. According to former Begin aides, the Prime Minister was furious at the 'gaffe' but amazed by Mengistu's reaction. After all, they argue, Israeli arms sales to Ethiopia were well known and had been reported in a number of African newspapers. They claim that Mengistu (under Russian pressure) used Dayan's statement as a convenient excuse to rid himself of any further obligation he might have felt towards Israel.

From the time Begin came to power in the summer of 1977 the Falashas were high on his agenda. During the short period of co-operation between Israel and Ethiopia in 1977, two groups amounting to 121 Falashas were brought 'legally' from Addis Ababa to Israel in Israeli military transport planes which had delivered arms to Ethiopia. After Dayan's leak, it became clear that other avenues would have to be explored.

There were growing pressures on Begin to formulate a policy. As the plight of the Falashas in Ethiopia became steadily worse, the involvement of the pro-Falasha groups in the United States and elsewhere grew. In January 1979, Rabbi Marc Tanenbaum compiled a report on the situation of the Falashas for the influential American Jewish Committee. He wrote that in the previous months 'several hundred Falasha were driven from their homes, others robbed of land and livestock, dozens murdered and still others sold into slavery'.

The indignation and concern of the Israeli Falashas expressed itself in the same month in a demonstration, encouraged by the AAEJ, in the square in front of the Israeli parliament building (Knesset). A week later a delegation of four Falashas was received by Prime Minister Begin. He was asked to evacuate the Ethiopian Jews by whatever means he could. He assured the Falashas that the government regarded them as Jews in every sense of the term and was committed to doing its best to help them. He promised them: 'We shall appeal to the Ethiopian government to let the Falashas go.' This clearly presented problems. Not only were there no diplomatic relations between the two states, but the new regime in Addis Ababa was particularly sensitive to any charge that the government was oppressing the Falashas. Was it not the previous feudal despotism which had oppressed the Falashas and had not the revolution been of positive benefit to them? The United States could not be expected to help either. Ethiopia was even to vote with the Soviet Union on Afghanistan and Soviet-style denunciations of the United States were becoming an almost daily occurrence. The prospects of co-operation were never very good, but by the end of 1979 it was clear that the Ethiopian government was not going to change its stance. The authorities did not allow any ethnic or religious group to leave Ethiopia and they were not prepared to make an exception in the case of the Falashas. In December 1979, Binyamin Avilea, an Israeli spokesman in the United States, conceded that attempts to persuade the Ethiopian government to let the Falashas go had failed. But a Falasha leader, Avraham Yardai, accused the Israeli government of not wanting the Falashas: 'It's the gates *here* that are closed, not in Ethiopia.'

By the late 1970s, Jewish organizations throughout the world had begun protesting against the lack of activity on the part of the Israeli government. The press began to take an interest in the Falashas. In February 1979, the *New Republic* carried an article, 'The Falashas: A Black Holocaust Looms', in which the impression was given that the Falashas were being liquidated and, like the Pygmies, would soon disappear. Further articles and news features appeared stressing that Jews were being killed and enslaved. Even some of Menachem Begin's supporters felt he was not doing enough for the Falashas. At an October 1979 conference of the Herut movement in London, an urgent appeal was made for Israel to do more for the Ethiopian Jews and to take all steps to facilitate their emigration to Israel. Within Israel, the Falashas and their supporters were increasingly becoming a force to be reckoned with. At the end of October 1979, Israeli Falashas staged another peaceful demonstration in front of the Knesset demanding large-scale emigration from Ethiopia. Shortly afterwards, representatives of the community met Begin and urged him to take some decisive action. Zacharia Yona, one of the Falasha leaders in Israel, said: 'We have nothing to lose by trying to make a fuss in public. If we keep quiet we may lose the whole community.'

For many, the *raison d'être* of the Jewish state was that it should offer a refuge to Jews in distress. Why not the Falashas? In 1979, the same year in which liberal Israel gave refuge to 400 Vietnamese boat people, there were only 350 Falashas in Israel. To many people this was incomprehensible. To Moshe Bar Yehuda, an official of Israel's Labour Federation, the explanation was simple. In an interview published in the *Los Angeles Times* in February 1979, he claimed: 'The first is prejudice – the colour of their skin. The government does not want them here. Secondly, the Israeli government doesn't want to endanger diplomatic contacts with African states.' The *Jewish Chronicle* ran a story, 'Save Falashas from Murder', in which Israeli Falashas accused Israeli officials of regarding their Ethiopian brethren as 'too primitive' and 'a potential burden'. The charge of racism was to be directed at the government time and time again. The Israeli paper *Davar* wrote: 'The Falashas have not come because they were not wanted. This is the simple truth and it must be stated.' In October 1979, the *Jerusalem Post* thundered that 'The Falashas ... have been neglected. And that neglect must be considered mortal.'

Something had to be done. Begin had been very alive to the Falasha problem since coming to power in 1977: he was in no sense bullied into an action of which he disapproved. Aides who worked with him at the time stress that the Falashas were always included on his daily agenda. He had a highly emotional attitude towards the 'ingathering' of Africa's black Jews and saw it in very much the same terms as the rescue of the remnant of European Jewry after the Holocaust. As one of his assistants put it, 'For Begin the Falasha cause had become a sacred duty of office.' Towards the end of 1979, Begin announced the formation of an inter-ministerial committee which had as its brief the co-ordination of the absorption of the Ethiopian Jews. It consisted largely of immigration and absorption officials and was not privy to some of the decisions on the 'rescue' that were taken at that time at a higher level. A couple of weeks later Begin pledged his government's co-operation with the recently formed Committee on Ethiopian Jews of the National Jewish Community Relations Advisory Council in the USA. Begin's cable read: 'We have done our utmost to save and bring the Jews of Ethiopia to our historic homeland, Eretz Israel. Every person of good will should support this campaign for this basic human right.' The Jewish Agency, in a dramatic shift from its previous policy of quiet diplomacy, called for a world-wide campaign to publicize the plight of the Falashas. Begin still maintained that the main thrust of his policy would be to influence the Ethiopian government. But already alternative ways were being examined.

In 1979, only five Falashas managed to get to Israel directly from Ethiopia. The official gates were closed. Thirty-two, however, reached Israel via Sudan, whose border with Ethiopia is only a hundred miles or so from the main concentrations of Falashas in Gondar. For the majority of Falashas, the only means of transport at their disposal was their feet. The only country they could walk to from Gondar was Sudan. So, caught in the cross-fire of military and political disturbance and feeling a growing conviction that Israel offered the only way out, the Falashas started to leave their traditional villages in the highlands and make their way to Sudan. There, in the vicinity of the dusty little market-town of Gedaref in the province of Kassala, refugee camps had already been established for the Christian refugees from Gondar who had been arriving since 1967. In the early part of 1977, Falashas began crossing regularly into Sudan and within three years there were hundreds of them swelling the growing number of refugees from war-torn Ethiopia. According to reports reaching Israel, their situation was not good.

Israel's influence in Africa generally had been severely reduced in the wake of the Yom Kippur War of 1973. Although Sudan had given tacit support to the Camp David peace treaty between Israel and Egypt and could not, therefore, be counted among the most relentless of Israel's enemies, none the less Israel wielded no influence in this Arab, Islamic state. Inevitably then, Israel would have to be cautious in its attempts to extricate the Falashas who were trapped there. The last thing the government needed was an international incident that would embarrass one of the more moderate Arab heads of state and at the same time harm Israel's attempts to regain credibility in Africa. On the other hand, Camp David had taken place in 1979 and President Sadat could perhaps be persuaded to use his influence with Sudan's President Numeiri. Operationally, the Sudan coast was within easy reach of Israel's southern shores on the Red Sea, particularly as in those days the Israelis controlled the Sinai coast right as far as Sharm el Sheikh. Connections were not too difficult to make, not least since Israeli *Resheph* missile boats were active in the Red Sea as far as Sudan and beyond. The mission was not, apparently, impossible, and the Mossad was well equipped to carry it out. There are many Mossad agents in Africa in a variety of guises. As a well-known Israeli journalist put it to me: 'We have BBC correspondents, Australian bushwhackers in Kenya, Cuban Jews with the Cubans in Ethiopia, others working with the British and French aid teams. We could send in Egyptian Jews, Yemenites or even Sudanese Jews. Best of all we had the Israeli Falashas who had a burning desire to help the rest of the tribe get out.'

One of the more impressive qualities of modern Israel lies in its ability to take bold and decisive action when it is seen to be necessary. Practical activism has become an important element in the character of the state and a down-to-earth readiness to act rather than to talk is one of the self-perceived virtues of the modern Israeli. This uncompromising belief in the power of action owes something no doubt to the Israeli view of Jewish submissiveness over the centuries. As Leon Wieseltier put it recently in a powerful article in the *New Republic*:

For centuries the Jews had dreamed of deliverance, but they were not delivered. Now they would become deliverers.... The proposition is that there is only one thing to be done about an emergency, and that is to end it; and that there is only one people that can be relied upon to end it, and that is your own.

Thus it was decided in February 1980 to entrust the operation of rescuing the Falashas to a section of Israel's redoubtable intelligence agency, the Mossad. Answerable in turn to the Prime Ministers Begin, Shamir and Peres, the Mossad has remained in control of the operation until now. For obvious reasons there are still operational aspects of the Mossad's involvement which cannot be revealed, and over the last five years there have been many demonstrations of personal valour on the part of Mossad agents which will have to go unsung for some years to come. From the earliest stages of operations the risks involved, not only for agents but also for the people they were trying to help, were enormous. Partly as a protective measure, the Israeli government adopted a policy of silence. Officially the operation was not taking place.

The Mossad operation was preceded by a diplomatic initiative. Both American diplomats and Begin asked Sadat to have a word with Numeiri about the Falashas. Sadat was successful in his approach and for some time Numeiri and the upper echelons of his secret service, the *AmnulDawla*, who were also involved, were prepared to turn a blind eye to discreet and relatively small-scale operations to remove the Falashas.

The Mossad was to co-ordinate activity within Sudan. In the early part of 1980, it was widely rumoured in Sudan that the second-in-command of the Mossad had visited Khartoum to establish a *modus operandi* with elements within the Sudanese state security service. At about the same time, according to Sudanese officials, a white man, working for the Mossad but claiming to be an aid official, came into the Khartoum offices of the Sudan Commission for Refugees. He said he had isolated a group of likely-looking workers in the refugee camps around Gedaref. These people, who happened to be Falashas, were clearly a burden on the Sudanese state, he said, and he would be happy to relieve them of that burden. He reached into his briefcase and pulled out work contracts for 400 people, along with a letter from a high-ranking official in the Kenyan Ministry of Information confirming that the men would be employed by a Kenyan company in the vicinity of Nairobi. His story seemed incredible to the Sudanese officials. After he left, they checked his credentials and discovered that he was not, in fact, a member of any aid organization. Subsequently, it is said, the man approached the United Nations High Commission for Refugees (UNHCR). According to Sudanese sources, certain UNHCR officials, particularly those in the Gedaref sub-branch, were prepared to co-operate. The UNHCR had been helping small groups of Falashas to leave Sudan for some years, although there were no official guidelines on the subject. The Khartoum head of UNHCR in 1980 was Ibrahim Saidi, an Egyptian who was an enthusiastic supporter of Camp David. During 1980 he was widely rumoured to be involved in facilitating the emigration of the Falashas.

A British development expert based in East Africa told me that he had met a group of American Catholic priests and brothers who were working with refugees in Kenya. According to them, since 1980 Falashas had been crossing into Kenya from Sudan. They stressed that the American embassy in Nairobi had instructed them not to talk about it. The operation was, they said, co-ordinated by the CIA and the Mossad with the active co-operation of the Kenyan authorities, who provided 'safe-houses' and other facilities. The Kenyans had been helpful to the Israelis at the time of the Entebbe raid and, according to a highly placed Israeli source, 'made no particular difficulties'. Kenya, after all, had more than its fair share of refugees from neighbouring countries and the last thing the government wanted was to be saddled with the responsibility of looking after Ethiopian Jews. The only proviso was that the operation should be shrouded in absolute secrecy. It was felt that to allow the Falashas to use the facilities of Nairobi International Airport and to allow them discreet transit facilities was no more than a humanitarian gesture. At the same time Kenya did not want to be thought of as party to an illegal, anti-Ethiopian plot to smuggle Ethiopian citizens out of Africa to 'racist', Zionist Israel. Kenya had good reason to wish to maintain good relations with Addis Ababa: Ethiopia was fighting a protracted war against Somalia, which for years had had designs on parts of eastern Kenya.

For some time the Falashas were able to use the Kenya route. The operation was run fairly effectively with the cooperation of a number of agencies. Jean-Claude Concolato, a young intellectual Frenchman who was running the Gedaref sub-office of UNHCR, did what he could to help the Falashas who passed through his office. The UNHCR did the first 'screening' of the Falashas, the International Catholic Migration Society (ICMS) was sometimes responsible for organizing the onward transport, the Sudan Commission for Refugees facilitated the issue of exit visas, and the Kenyans themselves issued entry visas and work permits, on the clear understanding that the latter would never be used. In the early years the Falashas, impatient to leave the camps, would sometimes try to organize their own transport to Kenya. Once or twice groups of them went to Concolato in Gedaref and asked his help in arranging overland transport to Kenya. He advised them against it, but some went anyway and managed to link up with the rail-head in northern Uganda. The majority, however, were flown from Khartoum airport in specially chartered planes which flew directly to Nairobi. From there they were flown straight to Israel.

There were a number of drawbacks to the Kenya route. It was of necessity a clumsy operation. Sudan, approximately the same size as India, is the biggest country in Africa. Nairobi is hundreds of miles south of the Falasha homelands. The problems of transport and concealment were immense. The Mossad was beginning to favour alternative routes when, in 1983, the Kenya route had to be abandoned. By then over 600 Falashas had been smuggled into Israel via Nairobi.

From the beginning of the operation the Mossad had been aware of the potential dangers represented by the extremely vocal and outspoken North American pro-Falasha groups: the American Association for Ethiopian Jews (AAEJ) and the Canadian Association for Ethiopian Jews (CAEJ). The last thing that was wanted was a group of inexperienced amateurs queering their pitch. A number of unofficial emissaries visited the North American groups to persuade them that Israel was taking action on behalf of the Falashas and that independent rescue missions were both unnecessary and harmful to the overall operation. On one occasion, Hirsch Goodman, a highly respected Israeli journalist, tried to explain to the Canadian group that every time they mounted a 'rescue' or revealed information about the general operation they were putting lives at risk. Completely unconvinced, they said that they had heard the same argument from a number of Israeli officials and that the discretion being urged upon them was no more than a ruse to conceal Israeli inaction. The AAEJ and CAEJ continued their activity and on more than one occasion ran into difficulties.

In mid-1983 an AAEJ-organized overland rescue got stuck in southern Sudan. Mossad agents were forced to help them out. But a few months later there was an even more dramatic failure. In October, two members of an independent rescue mission were arrested in Juba, a small town on the White Nile in eastern Equatoria, about 100 miles north of the Kenyan border. According to a Western relief worker who was in Juba at the time, they were both very naïve and completely unaware of the realities of Africa. They were arrested after a tip-off to the Sudanese police by a Zaire-based official of the UNHCR.

The story in a somewhat garbled form was picked up by the *Nairobi Standard*. The article read:

Through the co-operation of the Sudanese police, two whites, one called Tom and another Steven, were arrested after their aircraft, belonging to a reputable charter safari, was apprehended with six Ethiopians on board. In their possession were found several pictures and identification documents of other Ethiopians who have passed through their hands in recent times. The two whites admitted that they had no travel or entry documents for their passengers but said the Ethiopians under their charge were going for further studies. They did not know where the colleges they were going to were. At one time they thought the colleges were in America. But the irony of it was that most of the passengers were illiterate and others were beyond college-going years ... it was thought the Ethiopians were the Falasha, said to be black Jews, and are migrating into Israel.

The article further reported that the pair subsequently escaped into Zaire and that it was not known what had happened to the large sums of money in their possession. After high level American intervention, Mossad agents operating in Kenya were enabled to extricate the American Jews and their unfortunate charges. But this *débâcle* spelt the end of the Kenya route. The *Standard* article had disclosed routes ('crossing into Kenya through Malaba, Lortokitok, Moyale and Mandera'), names ('the racket had been organized by Mr Acklock Ferede, an Ethiopian who had stayed in Israel for a long time and then returned to Kenya and been issued with a passport by the Ethiopian embassy. ... He gave names of several people who had been travelling often across the borders to bring the Ethiopians into Kenya. They are Belay, Sheriffo, Beckle and his wife'), and methods ('the people have been hiring vehicles and aircraft from several tour companies and these details were available'). The Kenyan journalist, Barrack Otieno, had uncovered not only details of the 'private' operations but also some vital aspects of the Mossad's own routes and methods.

A further factor in the closing of the Kenya route was a product of the internal political situation in the country. One of the key figures in the Kenyan government and one who was thought to have the closest ties with the CIA and the Mossad, as well as the South African BOSS, was the Minister for Home and Constitutional Affairs, Charles Njonjo. A number of sources have indicated that Njonjo played a role in facilitating the passage of the Falashas through Kenya. But in the summer of 1983, he was arrested on charges of conspiring to overthrow the government in collaboration with Israeli and South African mercenaries. The climate in Nairobi became hostile for a while and it was decided that the Kenya route could no longer be used.

For some time Israel had been seeking ways of persuading the voluntary aid organizations to take a greater part in the operation. Relief organizations and even diplomatic missions in Sudan and Kenya had been bombarded by requests from Jewish organizations to help the Falashas. A Canadian human rights official in Nairobi claimed that nine-tenths of the letters he received from North America were on the subject of the Falashas. An American Jew was appointed director of an international organization in Khartoum in late 1981. Before he went out to Sudan, he was asked to participate in the rescue of the Falashas. In Khartoum he approached the Sudan Commissioner for Refugees, Ahmad Abdul Rahman, and asked for his help in facilitating the emigration of the Jewish refugees in the camps of eastern Sudan. Abdul Rahman refused on the grounds that, in his view, no special case should be made for any group.

Jean-Claude Concolato did not, however, hold this view and, during 1981, he was personally involved with the Falashas. 'Everything I did', he told me, 'was within the framework of our UN mandate to help refugees. I certainly did not feel that it was my duty to oppose attempts to remove the Falashas from Sudan. They were in a particularly vulnerable position. At the time we were trying to encourage self-sufficiency and integration as the guiding principles of refugee management: on both counts the Falashas were less able to manage than any other category of refugees. They were afraid of the Amhara refugees and they were afraid of the Sudanese police. The Falashas had been admitted as refugees into the country:

the prime responsibility of UNHCR was to protect them. I knew what was going on and I made no attempt to prevent it. My job was to protect these people and to help them as far as I could.' Concolato was, according to a volunteer who worked in his office in Gedaref, in an isolated position. He had difficult relations with his own Khartoum superior, a Swiss official called Müller who was wary of any UNHCR involvement, and he had at best the grudging support of certain members of his staff. UNHCR officials were divided on the issue of what ought to be done about the Falashas. There were those for whom the humanitarian aspect of the problem was paramount and there were those who could not ignore the political pitfalls involved in helping Jews emigrate from an Islamic country to Israel.

Concolato was aware of the urgency of the situation. By the middle of 1981, Um Raquba, the camp where the Falashas were chiefly concentrated, was in abysmal straits. The only recent refugees at the camp were Falashas and they were suffering from large-scale malnutrition. The rains had made the mud track joining the camp to Gedaref impassable, supplies in the camp had all but run out, and already over 160 Falashas had died.

The Frenchman felt that the position of the Falashas was substantively different from that of other refugees. In the first place, the Falashas were often attacked and even killed by other Ethiopian refugees who accused them of being responsible for all their ills. But even more significantly, unlike most of the other inmates of the camps, the Falashas had somewhere to go.

Other refugees were screened by the UNHCR for possible resettlement. But the number of them that could be accommodated by the United States, Canada or the other participating countries was pitifully small. The American resettlement scheme was the most generous one. Its original impetus had come from black pressure groups who wanted to encourage black immigration, at least in part to balance the number of Asian refugees entering the USA from South-East Asia. However, the United States quota for the whole of the African continent was only 3,000 people a year and the immigration criteria were stringent. The Canadians selected their immigrants from an even smaller pool. They only took computer technicians, doctors, university graduates and the like. The Swedes, for the most humane of reasons, had the most selective policy of all. They would only take physically handicapped refugees. Israel's immigration policy was simple. They would take all the Falashas: man, woman and child, the sick, the handicapped, as well as the young and able. A small country suffering from acute economic problems was prepared to take all 30,000 Falashas if they wanted to come. Like all other states Israel had its own immigration criteria: not that the incoming refugees should be an economic asset to the state, or that they should be sound or unsound of limb or mind, but simply that they should be Jews.

Concolato decided to fly to Geneva to try and persuade his head office to organize an immediate airlift of the Falashas to the one country which would take them. The UNHCR refused. Concolato became known to the Falashas in the refugee camps as someone who was prepared to help them and who would not report their clandestine activities to the Sudanese security forces. He helped them in a number of ways. Those who had been particularly badly treated on the border or within Sudan he tried to have placed on the lists of refugees destined for the American resettlement scheme. The Mossad at the time was arranging for regular groups of Falashas to travel to Khartoum, where they would first be accommodated in safe-houses and then be flown out on block visas either via Nairobi or Athens to Israel. The Falashas would travel by truck or in smaller groups on the normal passenger buses that connect Gedaref with the capital's central bus terminal at Suq al-Shab. As refugees were not allowed to travel to Khartoum without special authorization from the *AmnulDawla*, the Falashas would frequently be stopped and brought back to Gedaref where they were imprisoned. Concolato made it his business to get them released.

Often there was some sort of clearance, secured by bribes and other means, for the Falashas to travel to Khartoum, but the clearance had not been passed on to regional security and police officials. For aid workers like Concolato the situation was confusing. Messages from the *AmnulDawla* on the subject of the Falashas were always contradictory: no one seemed to know what was going on. In this difficult situation Concolato played a courageous role. Unaware of the full story, he did what he could to assist the black Jews under his care.

During 1981, two large groups numbering hundreds of Falashas were trucked from Gedaref to the Red Sea town of Suakin, a crumbling ghost town abandoned at the turn of the century when Port Sudan was developed as the country's chief port. From Suakin, which is not far from the American naval facility which has been there since 1979, they were transported by non-Israeli merchant ships to the Israeli town of Eilat at the northern end of the Gulf of Aqaba. The Falashas had been brought in small groups from Um Raquba to Te-wawa, a refugee camp two miles outside Gedaref, where by 1981 there were about 1,000 of them waiting to go to Israel. Concolato turned a blind eye to what was going on in the camps and did what he could to protect the Falashas from the Sudanese police.

In the course of the year a number of Concolato's Sudanese co-workers discovered that the Frenchman had been helping Ethiopian Jews to leave Sudan. At least one of his assistants resigned. Concolato had never made much of a secret of his views. In private conversations with his Sudanese colleagues he used to argue that it was hardly necessary for the Sudan to be more 'Arab' than Morocco, Algeria, Tunis, Libya, Egypt, Yemen, Iraq and the other Arab countries which had at one time or another let their Jews emigrate to Israel. Why should Sudan make a fuss about the black Jews of Ethiopia? His Sudanese colleagues were not convinced and finally Mr Ismail, then an Assistant Commissioner for Refugees, started writing reports for his government drawing attention to the emigration of the Falashas and requesting a policy directive on the matter. Although Numeiri and selected members of the *AmnulDawla* knew that the Falashas were leaving for Israel, and were even co-operating on certain points, the regional

branches of the Sudan Commission for Refugees were in no
sense privy to their counsels. The reports caused some embar-
rassment. Müller was furious that the UNHCR should be seen to
be involved at all and would subsequently never be prepared
to discuss the issue. At the end of 1981, Concolato, sick from
a variety of diseases contracted in Gedaref, left Sudan. It is
thought by many that he was asked to leave because of his
involvement with the Falashas. An Englishman who was
working for UNHCR at the time said of Concolato: 'Yes – he
was quite a hero.'

President Numeiri, never more than a lukewarm partici-
pant in the Falasha venture, and aware of the serious reper-
cussions the issue could have on Sudan's relations with the
Arab world, was disturbed by the reports arriving on his desk
from the Sudan Commission for Refugees. After the assassi-
nation of Anwar Sadat in November, he became less and less
inclined to close his eyes to the emigration of the Falashas. If
Anwar Sadat could be assassinated for his supposed 'modera-
tion' and collaboration with the Zionist enemy, so could he.
Thereafter Numeiri was a different man and, within two
years, Sudan had become a hard-line Islamic state.

There was, however, no clear-cut ban on Falasha emigration from Sudan and no firm policy directive from above. In
all the uncertainties and ambiguities that went to make up life
in Numeiri's Sudan, the Falasha question became one more
grey area. It was a situation in which the Mossad could continue to function.

Corruption at all levels of government was widely viewed
as being at the root of many of Sudan's problems. Foreign
contracts were only awarded against kick-backs and bribes of
all sorts were a part of daily life. People could be bought. In
addition, the administration of the country was chaotic. Ministers were frequently dismissed or reshuffled and had little
control over their ministries. They often had scant knowledge
of what was happening at lower levels. It was, therefore, possible to buy the services of civil servants with a degree of
assurance that their activities would not be discovered. At the
same time the government was held in contempt by the great

A group of Falashas standing in front of a *tukul* in the village of
Enda Bagona, Ethiopia, 1973

Falasha women selling their pottery at a local market, Taddä,
Ethiopia, 1973

A pottery figure of a Falasha carrying a child on the journey to Sudan

An Ethiopian refugee carrying a starving child, October 1984

After a long and difficult walk, with their possessions on their backs, a group of refugees cross the Sudanese–Ethiopian border, November 1984

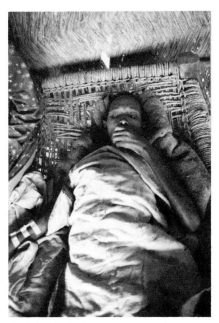

The entrance to the Reception Centre at the Um Raquba refugee camp, Sudan, November 1984

A dying Falasha woman receives medical treatment in Um Raquba, November 1984

Piles of stones mark the graves of Ethiopian Jews who made the long trek into Sudan, only to die before they could be rescued, November 1984

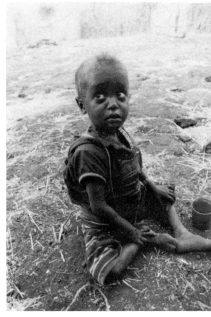

Falasha women and children in Um Raquba, November 1984

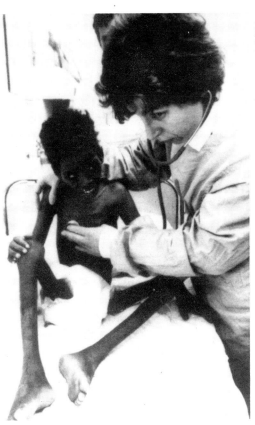

A twelve-year-old Falasha boy is examined in a Tel Aviv hospital after his arrival in Israel, January 1985

An Israeli volunteer teaches a group of orphaned Falasha children in Nahariya, January 1985

A cartoon by Dosh which appeared in the Israeli newspaper *Ma'ariv* after
Israel had been internationally congratulated for Operation Moses,
6 January 1985

Three days later, after accusations of Israeli indiscretion, the following
Dosh cartoon appeared in *Ma'ariv*

An Israeli welcomes an elderly Ethiopian Jew who has just arrived in Israel, January 1985

Young Falashas demonstrating in Jerusalem against the orthodox rabbinate's ruling that Falasha immigrants need to undergo a symbolic conversion on their arrival in Israel, January 1985

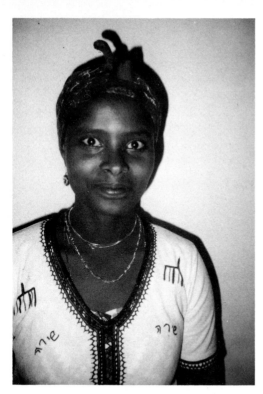

A young Falasha girl
photographed in Israel,
February 1985

A Falasha couple in their sparse
flat in a government absorption
centre, eleven months after
their arrival in Israel

majority of the population and to find people prepared to co-operate against it was not difficult. Highly placed Israeli sources insist that many Sudanese officials helped the Falasha operation out of a sense of moral conviction, which was often expressed in terms of traditional Islamic justice. Those that did not hold such views could be bought.

Money was needed on the ground in Sudan: to buy forged passports, to bribe officials to grant block exit visas and military units to keep away from sensitive areas. Most of all, money was needed to persuade the Sudanese security agents and officials to turn a blind eye to what was going on. Getting money into Sudan did not present any particular problem. There were a number of influential American and European Jewish businessmen with interests in Sudan and a sympathy for the Falasha cause. They were approached indirectly, sometimes by officials of international Jewish organizations, and asked to channel funds into the country. Non-Sudanese Arab *entrepreneurs* with financial interests in Sudan are said to have repaid past business favours by introducing considerable sums to key Sudanese officials. Between 1981 and the summer of 1984 millions of dollars were distributed in Sudan to ease the passage of the Falashas from the refugee camps near Gedaref to Khartoum and from there to a variety of destinations *en route* for Israel.

The money came directly from the Mossad's funds. It was not the first time that such funds had been used for buying Jews. The Second World War saw a number of examples of it. More recently, in the 1960s, the Poles were reportedly paid £30,000 for every Jewish family permitted to leave, and there were periods when the Romanians were paid considerable sums to permit Jewish emigration to Israel.

With this new situation the Mossad needed more people on the ground both in Ethiopia and in Sudan. Falasha and other operatives were dropped off the Sudan coast from *Resheph* missile boats and then made their own way to the refugee areas of eastern Sudan and into Ethiopia. The war in Eritrea and Tigre, as well as the onset of the drought, created near perfect conditions for the Mossad. War areas offer good cover for a variety of covert actions. The increasing population movements out of Tigre and Eritrea into Sudan offered excellent camouflage for the Falashas leaving Gondar and the various disturbances, particularly in the border areas, created disaffected groups who could be bought and used and who had little loyalty for either side.

In fits and starts the operation proceeded. Despite the considerable operational difficulties in Sudan the Mossad, working along with a number of international organizations and with the unofficial connivance of the UNHCR, succeeded by the end of 1982 in getting over 2,000 Falashas out of Sudan. During the period the Israeli government drew a veil of silence over the operation, and Israeli diplomats and civil servants discouraged any public speculation about the Falashas.

One consequence of this policy was that the Israeli government was beset by complaints from all over the Jewish world that they were mishandling the Falasha question. The complaints closest to home were those that came from the Israeli Falashas. In December 1981, a few dozen Falashas in Israel went on a protest march from Kibbutz Zova to the Knesset to stress their sense of identity with the Falashas of Ethiopia and to express their frustration at the government's efforts. They carried with them a petition of 38,000 signatures. One of the Falashas, Yitzhak Etgar, claimed that the Israeli government was doing nothing to help his compatriots: 'I have an elementary right to see my parents and my brothers', he insisted, voicing the desperation of the Israeli Falashas, practically all of whom had relatives in Ethiopia. Shortly afterwards, Yehuda Avner, now Israel's Ambassador to London but then a senior adviser to Prime Minister Begin, replied: 'For a long time the matter has been given high priority ... by the authorities under the personal supervision of the Prime Minister himself.' Avner stressed that claims to the contrary were 'a slander against the people and government of Israel, who consider the saving of Jews in distress a primary duty'. Unconvinced, a few months later 600 Falashas threatened to go on a hunger strike if nothing were done 'to counter the indifference of the Israeli authorities to the geno-

cide of their brothers', in the words of Simha Barhani, a
Falasha leader in Israel.

But nothing was said by the Israeli authorities to indicate
to the outside world that any practical steps had been taken
or that an 'escape route' had already been used. Israeli
government and Jewish Agency leaders came in for a great
deal of criticism, some of it violent. At an annual convention
of Jewish federations in Detroit, Menachem Begin, hardly the
darling of many American Jewish students anyway, was
abused and heckled by angry young Jewish students who accused him of 'betraying black Jews'. Begin said nothing and,
according to senior aides of his at the time, made sure that his
example was followed.

It was not long before the Jewish press was aware of the
presence of Falashas in refugee camps 'somewhere in Africa',
but Sudan was not yet explicitly mentioned. Israeli diplomats
did their best to keep any mention of Sudan out of the news.
In 1981 the American *National Jewish Monthly* carried an article by Howard Lenhoff, president of the American Association of Ethiopian Jews. He wrote:

Estimates are that at least 1,500 Falashas are in refugee camps in
African countries. I interviewed Falashas who had been in these
horrible camps – most for over a year, some for years. They told me
of high rates of disease and a lack of water, medical care and supplies. An Israeli doctor told me that the Falashas who come to Israel
have 'nineteenth-century diseases'.

The plight of Ethiopia's Jews attracted an enormous
amount of sympathy and expressions of solidarity from all
over the Jewish world, particularly North America. Indeed,
there have been few Jewish issues in recent times which have
generated as much feeling or have developed so potent a
mystique. This is partly because North American Jews, even
more than French or British Jews and certainly more than
Israeli Jews, inhabit a world very largely dominated by the
memory of the Holocaust and consequently feel acutely protective of any Jewish community which appears to be at risk.

And it is partly because the Ethiopian Jews are black. The Falashas' cause has thus represented an opportunity for American Jews to express liberal views which were sometimes more difficult to express in an American context, especially since American blacks had started counting the Jews (and Israel) among their political enemies. The Falashas – black, suffering Jews, persecuted in a distant (Marxist) land – moved the hearts of a broad cross-section of American Jewry in a particularly acute way.

The members of the AAEJ and the CAEJ took these feelings very much further. They developed an obsessive and exclusive interest in the Falashas, which frequently took the form of attacking Israel and which was more often than not accompanied by a measure of self-righteousness. By their constant and unwarranted use of slogans such as 'black holocaust' or 'Ethiopian genocide', they invoked and perhaps even exploited the Holocaust in a way that many Jews found offensive.

From the very beginning of the Israeli action in Sudan, the AAEJ created a background of incrimination and criticism. In February 1980 Nathan Shapiro, the then head of the Chicago chapter of the AAEJ, said: 'The Falashas are being slaughtered, tortured and sold into slavery in Ethiopia, yet the Israeli government will not do anything to help bring them to Israel.' In 1982 Graenum Berger, the bellicose founder of the AAEJ, told a meeting in New York that the Ethiopian Jews were facing 'a major holocaust' and that Israel was 'playing down their plight'. Another speaker said that the Falashas were 'the group of Jews most threatened today by potential genocide and most abandoned by the rest of the world'. The meeting determined to ask the Israelis why they were 'turning a deaf ear' to the plight of black Jews. Shapiro argued frequently at press conferences and elsewhere that the Israelis' silence was due merely 'to those in the government who do not want to accept the Falashas as Jews'. Howard Lenhoff accused Jewish Agency and Israeli Foreign Office officials (specifically Yehudah Dominitz and Moshe Gilboa) of doing everything in their power 'to sabotage any significant movement of Falashas to

Israel'. Gratuitously he added, 'Those bureaucrats have cushy jobs and they know it.' Shapiro, now the newly elected president of the AAEJ, claimed that between May 1982 and March 1983 'only 150 Falashas have been brought to Israel. At that rate it will take a dozen years to clear out the refugee camps. And what about the 20,000 Falashas in Ethiopia?' Armed with powerful rhetoric and a burning sense of commitment, the AAEJ did its best to arouse public opinion. US senators, such as Rudy Boschwitz, and congressmen, such as Tom Lenthos and Stephen Solarz, were enlisted by the AAEJ to help the Falasha cause. In 1983 the City Council of Chicago, one of the great centres of AAEJ activity, was persuaded to sponsor a strong resolution on behalf of the Falashas which was sent to President Reagan.

The Falasha organizations continued to steal the limelight and to underscore the apparent inactivity of the Israeli government. In March 1983, the Public Council for Falasha Jews meeting in Jerusalem announced that the American Council for the Falashas would help establish a settlement for the Ethiopian Jews in the mountains near Jerusalem. At about the same time, the Falasha organizations started disseminating reports that the condition of the Falashas was bad and that some of them were actually starving to death. These reports coincided with an announcement from Knesset member Mordechai Porat that the following Passover the Falashas would get their matza supply from Israel. The American Jewish *Sentinel* ran the two stories together without comment. Shapiro kept up his attacks. 'Three thousand Jews face death in African refugee camps but the US Congress and Jewish organizations abroad are being told by Israel to keep quiet,' he announced at a press conference in Tel Aviv. He said that since 1979 some Ethiopian Jews had been rescued from the camps, but it was not nearly enough. His organization had been forced to participate in the rescue attempts. Acknowledging that the Israeli government had been critical of its activities, he promised that his committee would discontinue direct rescue work if the Israeli government would play a more active role. He stressed that the government had only taken sporadic action and that what was needed was a sustained and massive effort. Shapiro said that the Jews would die of starvation, disease or at the hands of other Ethiopian refugees within the next two years unless immediate action were taken.

A film made by Simha Jacobivici, one of the most outspoken of the American-based activists, claimed that the only impediment to Falasha emigration was Israeli 'racism'. A Sudanese minister was interviewed in the film and stressed that, as far as he was aware, there were no difficulties in the way of Falashas wanting to leave Sudan: the only problem was Israeli's reluctance to take them. The hostile atmosphere generated by the AAEJ and later the publicity surrounding the film finally goaded the Israeli authorities into a reaction. One spokesman said: 'Thousands are on the way – the process is on. But it gets blocked up by these self-righteous people who don't care if a thousand are lost, just as long as they can say that they saved a hundred people while Israel did nothing.'

Suffering from international odium as never before as a result of the invasion of the Lebanon, the government found the incessant sniping from the Falasha groups a great irritant. The official argument, which was that Israel was doing her best but that absolute secrecy must be maintained, was not a persuasive one. For a time Israeli officials tried to bypass the AAEJ by recognizing a less aggressive pro-Falasha group as the 'official organization in the United States representing the Ethiopian Jews'. They favoured the newly formed North American Conference on Ethiopian Jews, which had already demonstrated a less critical and aggressive stance. This ploy had no noticeable success.

The greatest nuisance of the AAEJ and the CAEJ came not from their criticisms of Israeli policies but rather from their independently mounted rescue missions. These private initiatives started in 1980 when the AAEJ was responsible for flying twenty-two Falashas from Khartoum to Frankfurt. Some of these had been smuggled out of Sudan by an Ethiopian Christian who had been paid $2,000 a head to deliver his charges to Frankfurt. According to Graenum Berger, the Jewish

Agency refused to accept some of the group as Jews. One of the young men returned to Khartoum and subsequently committed suicide, and six of them stayed on in Germany in dubious circumstances. The rest of the twenty-two were flown on to Israel. Thereafter, nearly all these private initiatives operated either through Kenya, in some cases directly from Ethiopia, or directly from Ethiopia to Israel. In November 1981, Henry Rosenberg, a vice-president of the AAEJ, was responsible for smuggling out fourteen Falashas from Ethiopia, some of whom he accompanied as he flew from Addis Ababa via Cairo to Tel Aviv. Normally very few Falashas were taken out at a time, often in small locally chartered planes. By the middle of 1983, the AAEJ claimed to have brought out a total of 104 Falashas and, between then and the end of 1984, it is thought that they brought out another forty or fifty. It must be said that the volunteers who undertook these missions were courageous and committed people who put themselves at considerable personal risk. None the less, they did very much more harm than good.

Some of their operations failed on the ground and had to be rescued by Mossad operatives, who in at least one case had to break cover to do so. Other missions succeeded in 'rescuing' Christian Ethiopians, who had passed themselves off as Falashas in order to get out of Ethiopia. But their greatest nuisance value was that they created unwanted publicity and focused media attention on the overall operation. Towards the end of 1981, an article in the Miami *Herald* gave away delicate information; the article in the Nairobi *Standard*, which has already been mentioned, effectively closed the Kenya route; and an article in the *Observer* in July 1983 threatened to stop the whole operation.

The *Observer* article was written by a respected journalist who picked the story up in Sudan, where it was already well known in Western relief circles thanks in part to the indiscretions of the AAEJ volunteers, particularly those who had been arrested in Juba. Richard Hall's story read:

An underground network is channelling the Falashas, the 'black Jews' of Ethiopia, out of their homeland to become settlers in Israel. The network is largely financed by Jewish pressure groups in the United States and Canada. The operation is being conducted in the greatest secrecy because the Falashas' only escape route is through the Sudan, an Islamic country. Some of the emigrants are taken out by air from Khartoum; others are thought to have left by boat from the small Sudanese port of Suakin, sailing up the Red Sea to Eilat. . . .

A key role in this campaign has been played by the American Association for Ethiopian Jews, founded by Graenum Berger. . . . The Falashas are lured to cross into the Eastern Sudan with promises that they will at last be able to leave for the 'land of milk and honey'. They stay in refugee camps around Gedaref until they can be 'ferried' onwards. At one time there were three thousand of them in the camps.

The tone of the article is clearly anti-Zionist. Hall now admits that he had little evidence for his allegation that the Falashas were 'lured' out. But Israeli diplomatic circles were alarmed for other reasons. Their activities in Sudan had been uncovered. Shortly after the publication of the *Observer* article, an AAEJ worker compounded his organization's clumsiness by making a threatening telephone call to Hall. Normally nothing could be more calculated to encourage a newspaperman to get his teeth into a follow-up story than threats of this sort. Fortunately, Hall left his story at that and no one else picked it up.

The mishaps that befell the AAEJ became embarrassingly well known. As an *Economist* article (12 January 1985) put it: 'Some came to grief either while moving their charges through Europe, because their papers were not in order, or before they left Africa. A courier working under the name of "Jack Charity" was arrested in southern Sudan in 1983 with a small group of Falashas.' American Jewish opinion started to turn sharply against the AAEJ. One commentator remarked gently but effectively:

For just as it is eternally true that if we save a single life, it is as if we have saved the entire world – it is equally and immediately true that if, through indiscretion, we lose a single life, it is as if we have lost the entire world.

Any criticisms implying that the AAEJ were creating difficulties for the Israeli operation fell on deaf ears. AAEJ members continued to argue with some self-satisfaction that if they could get Jews out of Ethiopia with their slender resources and only amateur operatives, why could the State of Israel with unlimited funds and the Mossad at its disposal not get out the whole of the Falasha population? Criticisms that AAEJ members were anti-Israel were sharply rejected. In 1983 in a letter on file in a number of Jewish archives, Graenum Berger wrote:

I have probably raised 15 to 20 million dollars for Israel and its institutions over the span of my lifetime. We are responsible for a swimming-pool in the Jerusalem WYHA which bears our name. We gave Teddy Kollek and the Jerusalem Foundation $7,500 to establish a playground for children in Liberty Bell Park in Jerusalem in 1982. So when I am, like Lenhoff and others, charged with being anti-Israel and using the Falashas as my excuse for upbraiding it, I defy any of my critics to have as good a record. Politically I am a hawk and I wouldn't have given a grain of Sinai sand back to Egypt, nor would I give the West Bank, nor would I get out of Lebanon, until every Syrian and PLOnick gets out of that country. . . .

By the end of 1982, there were 2,500 Ethiopian Jews living in Israel, the great majority of whom had been brought from Sudan via the network established by the Mossad. Throughout 1983 groups of Falashas continued to be brought out of Khartoum on a number of European airlines, flown to Europe and then taken on to Israel. Throughout 1983 1,800 Falasha refugees left Sudan by this route. Fully aware of the need to clear the refugee camps as quickly as possible, the Israelis decided to try a more direct operation. A few miles north of Gedaref, near a small town called Showak, there is a small 1,000-metre desert air-strip. It was the closest air-strip to the main concentrations of Falashas in the refugee camps

at Tewawa and Um Raquba, but only serviceable during
the dry season. One night in July two unmarked Hercules
transport planes landed at the strip. They landed at night for
reasons of secrecy, but also because the cooler night air tem-
perature permits of a shorter runway requirement for landing
and take-off. But even so, taking off from a 1,000-metre strip
requires skilful flying and military, rather than civil, operational procedures must have been followed. Each plane picked
up a full capacity load of 200 refugees, who had been brought
there from the camps by truck. There were apparently some
delays in take-off because the planes were clearly seen by local
residents. Some of them suspected that the planes were part
of an Ethiopian raid on Sudan. Police units raced to the scene
too late to stop the planes and, for the next few days, the
police carried out somewhat dilatory interrogations in the
Falasha quarters of the camps. They discovered nothing. It is
clear that these operations were carried out with the connivance of the Sudanese *AmnulDawla*. It is said that no Israeli
personnel were used on the operation. Indeed, throughout the
entire operation in Sudan the Mossad went to great lengths
to ensure that no traces of Israeli involvement should ever be
discovered. This same method was to be used in March 1984,
when again two Hercules landed near Gedaref. This action
was still a frequent topic of conversation in Sudan six months
later. The first landings at Showak were later referred to in
the AAEJ literature as 'the great Israeli rescue of mid-1983'. In
all, 2,213 Falashas managed to get to Israel in 1983 and, using
the same more or less discreet methods, by September 1984 a
total of 6,000 Ethiopian Jews had gone to Israel. Falashas
were frequently seen by travellers on Air France and Swiss
Air flights from Khartoum, and on other carriers such as
Olympic Airways and El Al, bound for Israel's Ben-Gurion
Airport. Travellers who used the same flights have reported
that the Falashas were escorted by 'middle-aged American
matrons' or 'bearded European men'. By the end of 1983, this
aspect of the operation was working smoothly. The Falashas,
for the most part, were treated like any other refugees who
had been accepted by a host country for resettlement. There

were two differences. Unlike resettlement refugees, the Falashas left the airport in the rags they had worn in the camps
and they were given block transit visas rather than visas to
host countries. Four European countries co-operated in this
respect. Exit visas were obtained in the normal way through
the emigration authorities, while 'Joshua' co-ordinated the
various organizations concerned and the internal transport
arrangements required to move the Falashas from the camps
to the international airport in Khartoum. If the Sudanese
were not very enthusiastic about this arrangement, they had,
at any rate, been persuaded to go along with it. As a result,
the Falashas were being moved at a faster rate than ever
before. It seems clear that American pressure applied from the
highest levels was responsible throughout 1983 for ensuring
the smooth continuation of the programme.

By 1984, it became clear to everyone concerned that the
operation was running into difficulties. The Falashas had, over
the previous three months, been crossing into Sudan in large
numbers. The conditions in all the camps were horrific, but
particularly so in Um Raquba where most of the Falashas
were. The Sudanese felt there was a limit to what could be
expected of them; none the less they agreed to a greatly
accelerated movement of Falashas through Khartoum. Sometimes groups of 200 Falashas were seen on passenger flights
arriving in Israel. In the twelve months before Operation
Moses thousands of black Jews arrived on regular flights at
Ben Gurion Airport in Lod. But this was no longer enough.

CHAPTER SIX

The Flight from Gondar

The deliberations in Jerusalem and the gradual formulation
of a Falasha policy were not directly related to the exodus of
the Falashas which started in the late 1970s. Why did they
leave? This is the question that I put to Falashas I met in the
refugee camps of Sudan and those I met later in Israel. Yitzhak, an old Falasha I met in one of the refugee camps near
Gedaref, who had left Gondar three years before, told me:
'One day in 1979 a rumour started going around that there
was a road through the desert which would take us to Jerusalem. We came here to Sudan because we want to go to
Israel. We had always dreamed of Jerusalem. First of all I
sent my son from the mountains to see if there was a way to
the Holy Land. He went away and six months later he sent
me a letter. He told us that he had reached Jerusalem and
that if we crossed the mountains and came down into the
Sudan we would be able to go to Jerusalem too. I took my
wife and sons and daughters and I came to this place. Now I
am waiting to go to Jerusalem.' He spoke these words calmly
and patiently. 'Did you not come because of the famine?' I
asked. He smiled: 'In my life I have seen much famine. Some
years there is food, some years there is none. Also there is no
food here,' he gestured at the camp around us. 'No, we came
here because the time has come for us to join our people in
Israel.' Two months later I spoke to a young Falasha who
had come to Israel in 1979. He explained: 'I dreamed of
coming to Jerusalem all my life. I thought it would be different. I thought we would pray all day long in Jerusalem and
be dressed in white.' We were standing on a low hill in Yemin
Moshe overlooking the old city of Jerusalem. He pointed at

the city: 'The real Jerusalem is more beautiful than in my dreams – but our life is less beautiful. We have to work and study. It is more like Addis Ababa than Jerusalem.'

I asked an old Falasha from a remote village in the Semien mountains how he had come to hear of Israel. He was nonplussed by the question and a little aggressive. 'It is written in the Torah that Israel is our home. We have always known about Israel. We are the descendants of Abraham, Isaac, Jacob, Moses and Solomon. Like the other Jews we have been waiting for many years. For hundreds of years. A few years ago we heard that Israel had become independent and that the Jewish state was fighting wars and defeating its enemies just like the Beta Israel in Ethiopia used to fight wars and defeat their enemies. Finally we left the place to which we were exiled and like the other Jews, like the white Jews, we came home.' Much the same reasons can be heard from more recent immigrants.

'Why did we leave Ethiopia?' repeated a beautiful seventeen-year-old girl who had just arrived in Israel. 'We left Ethiopia because we wanted to come to the Land of Israel – to Jerusalem. For three weeks we walked through the mountains. We only walked at night. I became ill with malaria and my friends carried me to Sudan on a stretcher made with branches. Every night I prayed as we walked along, "O God! Let us get to Jerusalem. Let us get to Israel!" Some of us died on the way but many of us are here.' An old man who had come by the same route joined in: 'Yes, we all prayed that we might have the blessing of getting to Jerusalem.' He murmured a Falasha prayer:

> 'Do not separate me, O Lord, from Thy chosen people,
> From the joy,
> From the light,
> From the splendour.
> Let me see the light of Israel, O Lord.'

'When the plane came down in Israel,' he continued, his face alive with the memory, 'we saw the light of Israel. There were so many lights!'

These were the stories I heard in the camps of Sudan and in the absorption centres of Israel. According to their own account, the Falashas were drawn to Israel by an ancient and powerful love for a place that they had never seen and about which they knew little. It is openly said in Israel that the Falashas are the last Zionists. The Russian Jews want to leave Russia very much more than they want to go to Israel: many of those that have left the USSR have preferred to go to the United States. The Jews of America and Western Europe are happy to be Zionists at a distance. The Falashas are the real thing. They argue that they left their homeland primarily because of their love of Zion.

Strong Zionist sentiment had existed among the Falashas for some time. In 1974 a Jewish journalist visited the Falasha villages and reported that 'for days the major topic of conversation was Israel and *aliya* [immigration to Israel]. They had hundreds of questions relating to jobs, transport and the army (they all want to serve). The desire to immigrate is intense.' The journalist was asked by a Christian missionary working in the area: 'What's with these people? Each man's sole dream is to bring his family to Israel – a place they know little about and have never been to.' As the situation of the Falashas deteriorated throughout the 1970s, a sense of messianic expectation gradually began to infect them in much the same way as it had in 1862, when so many of them had perished in the land around Axum on their ill-fated march to Jerusalem. In 1862 they had decided to flee Ethiopia because they feared for their survival as a people; from the late 1970s, the survival of the tribe as a separate entity was again under threat. Now they started their descent from the mountains of Gondar to the plains of Sudan. From the beginning of 1977, Falashas started crossing into Sudan in small groups and by 1979 there were hundreds of them in the refugee camps.

The Zionism of the Falashas received some encouragement in the spring of 1980 when a handful of Israeli Falashas, recruited by and working with the Mossad, returned to the Falasha villages by a variety of routes and let it be known that the moment for which the black Jews had been waiting so long had arrived. They brought the welcome tidings that their people would gain immediate citizenship if they could get to Israel and that the Israelis had promised to help them get there from Sudan. All they had to do was reach Sudan. The Falashas did not need much persuading. The Ethiopian government was later to claim that the Falashas had been 'forced and enticed' across the border by 'counter-revolutionary and Zionist groups'. If they were enticed, then they needed little enticement. The only force that was employed was that used by the Ethiopian authorities in trying to prevent the Falashas from leaving the country.

The dreadful political situation in the late 1970s was in part responsible for awakening their latent Zionism. Their plight was so bad and was deteriorating so rapidly that they had every motivation to leave; and Israel was the only place to which they could go. At the same time, Ethiopia was becoming the scene of tremendous population movements created by the political disturbances within the country as well as by the drought and famine. Migration and movement were in the air. Many of the motives for the general migration exercised the Falashas too. At the same time, they were able to use the mass movement of people to conceal their own specific intentions: to get to Israel.

Although the famine has still not hit Gondar as hard as some other areas of Ethiopia, from early 1982 the drought had become a serious factor in the province. The pasture was all but lost; thousands of head of cattle died; the crops began to fail. A Falasha I met in Um Raquba refugee camp, who had left Gondar in early 1984, told me that he had left for two reasons: he wanted to go to Jerusalem and, in addition, his crops had failed. Collecting together what remained of the previous year's harvest, he joined eighty other Falashas from his village and left for Sudan. A Falasha who had left the Semien region two years before told much the same story. 'When the revolution came they gave us land. We were happy to have the land because we had never owned our land in the past. But the drought came to the mountains and there was no rain. For a whole year there was no rain. Our lands were no good to us. That is why we wanted to leave our village and come to Israel.'

According to the American Jewish Joint Distribution Committee, by the autumn of 1984 some half a million people in Gondar faced starvation as a result of the drought. Two Seattle doctors who visited the Gondar area in November 1984 said that starvation had not yet come to the province, but that if the crops failed again there would be mass starvation by the spring of 1985. Clearly, when the Falashas left Gondar, the prospects were not good.

The Falashas from the remote Semien villages on the borders of Tigre suffered more from the drought than those nearer to Gondar. A researcher for the International Disaster Unit came across a large group of Falashas in Wad Sherifat, a refugee camp near Kassala in eastern Sudan. They did not admit that they had left their villages because of the drought. The official I spoke to, who prefers not to be named, said: 'These people had nothing. They were the poorest of the poor. I never saw poorer refugees in Ethiopia or Sudan. First they had made a great trek north, for hundreds of miles, in search of work, then they turned left and marched towards Kassala. When they arrived they were more dead than alive.'

In many cases the Falashas were driven from their villages by peasants from the north who were themselves fleeing the drought. Often such refugees would take over the land of Falashas who had already left for Sudan and would then start encroaching on the land and property of those who remained behind. The Falashas were unable to protect themselves and by now the local authorities were in no mood to do anything for them. Their houses and synagogues were burned down or taken over, their cattle and other animals were stolen, their lands expropriated; they were left with no choice but to join the other members of the villages who had made the long trek. In late 1983 the crops in some Falasha villages fell prey to fighters of the Tigre People's Liberation Front, who had managed to sustain intense military activity against the government forces for the previous few months.

The fear of conscription was an added incentive for Falashas to leave their villages. The deteriorating military situation in the north and the heavy losses experienced by government forces led the Dergue to extend conscription to even the most remote villages. A British aid worker who was in Tigre told me that she had spent some weeks with a group of Falashas who had left Debarek in north Gondar chiefly out of fear of conscription. 'Their desire to go to Israel was genuine enough. They had heard it was a good place to go. But they had a great fear of conscription and the drought looters.' Their fears were not unfounded. A young Falasha called Abebe, whom I met in Gedaref, told me that whereas conscription was not directed specifically against the Falashas, once a Falasha had been conscripted he would never be returned to his home village. He would be taken to the front with Somalia and there he would stay. 'It is the government's latest way of solving the Falasha problem. Sometimes if a Falasha has been very badly wounded in the war they will let him come back – but only if he is too badly injured to walk.'

In addition to the drought, the fear of looters and the military draft, the exodus began to take on its own momentum. Many of the younger and stronger members of the villages had already left Gondar and had been successful in getting to Sudan or even to Israel. The visitors who travelled to the Falasha villages between 1982 and 1984 commented on the fact that there were hardly any young men left. A visitor to Wolleka, in 1983, mentioned that there were simply no men at all between the ages of eighteen and thirty-five in the village and the same was true in many other villages throughout Gondar. As the boys left behind grew older, they wanted to join their older brothers and fathers in Sudan and Israel. Dawit, a Falasha boy interviewed by a Jewish traveller in 1983, said: 'I am strong and I know I can get there, to that place over the mountains and across the border. There is a country where I know many Falashas are. Some day we can go to Israel. I cannot live here any longer. I must take care of my brothers and sisters, and they are very young. We are hungry. We have no *birr* [money]. I must go soon.' As the exodus progressed, news of the successful treks across the mountains was brought back to the remaining Jewish villagers by the Falasha emissaries working for the Mossad. The Falashas who had made it to Israel wrote to their families and friends urging them to come too. By early 1984 the trickle turned into a flood.

Why did the Falashas leave? The famine, the wars and the years of oppression all played their part. But perhaps the most important factor was the sense that their community had come to the end of the road and that their existence and ultimate 'redemption', political and religious, could only be assured by going as a community to the promised land. As more and more Falashas were successful in getting to Israel over the years, those that were left behind were spurred on to follow them.

The decision to leave was not taken lightly. There were great deliberations and discussions in the villages for weeks before the groups set off. Aware of many of the dangers that lay before them, the Falashas made what preparations they could. The planning sessions took place at night and were conducted secretly. Food for the journey had to be hoarded, water carriers had to be collected. A few villagers were able to get hold of medicaments, particularly against the malaria which they knew would be a danger once they left the mountains. One by one, groups from the hundreds of villages scattered throughout Gondar province set out. In some cases whole villages left together led by Israeli Falashas working for the Mossad. Elsewhere the youngest and fittest went, leaving the old and very young behind. The individual stories of courage and dogged determination have an epic quality as impressive as anything else in the Falashas' long history.

One young Falasha woman I met in Israel told me her version of this modern exodus. 'When I first left my village in order to come to Jerusalem I was fifteen. A Falasha had come to our village and told the elders that we could walk to Jerusalem. We had a meeting and the elders told us what they had heard. They said that it was written in our holy books that one day we should go to Israel and that the time had now come. I set out with my brothers and sisters and some friends. My brother had brought malaria pills from the clinic in Gondar. We had water in plastic carriers, a supply of *injera* [flat porous bread], and the clothes we had were the *shamma* we were wearing. At one o'clock in the morning we left our village in the Semien mountains and crept out like thieves. For two nights we walked and in the day we slept. On the second morning soldiers found us and took us by truck to their army camp. We were questioned by an officer and my brothers were beaten. The soldiers wanted to have me, but the officer would not let them. We were accused of being Zionist spies and leaving for Israel. We told them that we were travelling to look for work, but they did not believe us. We were put in prison and stayed there for six months. We were all tortured, but it was worse for my brothers. When we were let out of prison we were taken back to our village. We stayed there for three weeks, but then we decided to try and leave again. This time we made our plans even more carefully. Our parents wanted to come with us, but they had been warned that the journey to Sudan was very difficult and that many had died. They decided to stay behind, but told us that we must go to Jerusalem. They gave us their blessing and told us that God would protect us. When we left there was no moon. My father walked with us as far as the next village. Then he returned home. This time our group was larger because all the younger ones in the village had decided to go. There were some older ones too. When we started off from the village we were twenty-eight people. We travelled for three nights and then rested in a Falasha village. Most of the young people in that village had already left and the older ones had decided that they would leave the following week. They killed chickens and made some good food for us. The following day we were captured by soldiers, who beat the men and did other things to two of the girls.' As she said this she hung her head in shame and it was some time before she was able to carry on with her story.

'That night we escaped. We walked for about a week. For some of the way we had a Christian guide who showed us the path over the mountains. But he left us. The next day we were

captured by *shiftas*. The men wanted to fight, but they had
no guns. The *shiftas* threatened to kill us, but we pleaded with
them and they took our food, our ornaments, our clothes and
also the malaria pills which my brother had brought for us.
They took the amulets against the evil eye which the children
wore around their necks. They did not take our water carriers.
We walked for another ten days. The older ones were unable
to carry on and we had to leave them. They said they would
try to return to the village. I left my uncle and aunt by the
side of the track. We all cried. Some of the children died on
the way. My sister had a baby. It was born early and was
very small. The men carried her for a week on a stretcher
until she was strong enough to walk. We hardly had any water
and we had no *injera*. We ate berries that we found along the
way. We were walking barefoot. Some of us had set off with
shoes and the *shiftas* had stolen them. Our feet were bleeding
from the stones and thorns. We walked at night and could not
see the way. Often we lost the path and had to turn back. We
had long sticks which we used so that we would not stumble.
My brother and his friend became ill and died. I think they
had malaria. But my brother had been badly beaten and was
very weak. We had to leave them there, we were too weak to
bury them. We piled some stones and branches on the bodies
but we were not able to cover them properly. We were starving.

'One night we were resting by a big rock and a man came
up to us. He was a Falasha, but not from our village. He was
a tall, strong man. He was not starving. He gave us food and
water and some of us medicine. He showed us the way to go
and told us that people were waiting for us and would take us
to Jerusalem. When we were on the right path he left us. He
was going up the mountain to help other Falashas leave. We
walked for two more days and then we came to the border
with Sudan. The soldiers were waiting for us. They took us
on a lorry to Um Raquba, where we found many Falashas
from other villages. Of the twenty-eight who left, eight died
on the way and four turned back. Every night as we walked
we prayed that God would bring us to Jerusalem.'

Many of the Jews came to Sudan in better organized groups led by Falasha guides who knew where to find the stores of food, water and medicine which had been carefully hidden along the secret paths by Mossad agents. The couriers were Israeli Falashas, trained by the Mossad, who for years had gone back and forth to Gondar by two or three set tracks across the mountains. They were often helped by young Falashas, recently arrived from Gondar, who returned to help other villagers leave. Two of the main routes followed the Angereb river and, further to the north, the Takkaze. There were frequent diversions to avoid settled areas and army posts.

An aid official who was working in Um Raquba at the time told me: 'The Falashas arrived in a rather bad state. They were generally worse off than the other refugees and, according to the accounts they gave, rather more than ten per cent of them died on the way. Usually it was the older women and children who died on the journey. Some died of malaria, some were bitten by snakes, some were shot by government forces or attacked by other refugees. Some of the women had been raped by *shiftas* or government troops. Often they had run out of food. However, unlike the other refugees, most of them turned up with yellow plastic water containers which in some cases still had water in them. The clothing of the Falashas was usually in a worse condition than that of the other refugees and the children had very little clothing at all. They all arrived carrying long sticks which they had used to stop themselves stumbling on the mountain tracks. They had only walked at night because they were afraid of being attacked by the Ethiopian air force.'

Usually the Falashas left their villages with whatever they thought they might need for the journey and nothing else. Their babies and provisions were carried in animal-skin slings on their backs. But the communities also brought their books and manuscripts. The priests had carried their religious books with them, some of which, along with a collection of ancient Falasha manuscripts flown out of Sudan on Operation Moses, are now being examined by a committee of experts in Jerusalem.

The 'organized' groups had usually included Falashas of all ages. Entire villages came – very old people as well as babes in arms. But, at the same time, there were constant arrivals of smaller groups of young people who had found their own way across the mountains and even of individuals who had joined larger groups of Ethiopian refugees and had passed themselves off as Christians.

Sometimes on the border, the Sudanese army patrols refused to let them cross. A Falasha who had come over with his entire village, travelling with a large group of Christians from another area, told me that they had had to wait at the border for three days. 'As we had been such a large group we had not been attacked by *shiftas* and we had some money and other valuables. But we had no food or water. For three days we waited without food or water. Many died at the border. Then we gathered together all the *birr* that we had and gave it to the officer. He took the money and when night came he let us cross into Sudan. We walked for two more days and found our way to Um Raquba.'

Those who were not fortunate enough to have a Falasha guide would occasionally be able to find a Christian guide, sometimes a professional smuggler, who would take them across the mountain passes for a payment which was often as much as $100, a great deal of money in a country where the average per capita income is $140 per annum. The deal reached with many guides was that they would take their charges over the mountains in the direction of Grar Wiha and leave them at the Atbara river just before the border with Sudan. Others were taken to the Atbara from further north, by-passing the small border town of Abderafi. Not all the guides were reliable. Some Falashas told me that they had been deserted by their guides once they had received their payment. Other guides 'sold' their charges to *shiftas* or Ethiopian army units.

The difficulties that the Falashas experienced getting out of Ethiopia can scarcely be overstated. They crossed hundreds of miles of some of the most difficult terrain in Africa, travelling at night to avoid army and rebel units and gangs of *shiftas*.

Some travelled for weeks, some for months. They passed through areas of rebel activity and, in some cases, virtual war zones. Those that came down from the mountains in the winter, as many of them did, had to ford raging mountain streams in the dark. As they left the highlands they were decimated by measles, dysentery and malaria. They all suffered terribly from hunger and thirst. The traumas of the journey stayed with some of them long after they had arrived safely in Sudan and will not be forgotten. Like the exodus of the Israelites from Egypt, the migration of the Falashas from Ethiopia is a mixture of tragedy and heroism which should stand as a monument to their determination to create a new future in the Land of Israel.

CHAPTER SEVEN

Not Jerusalem

Um Raquba, the camp to which most of the Falashas went, is about twenty miles from the border. In Sudanese Arabic the name means 'mother of shelter'. The plain between the hilly border country and the refugee camp was, by 1984, a stony desert which many of the Falashas had crossed by foot. When they arrived at the camp the Falashas were hungry, in some cases starving, thirsty and ill. After the traumatic march from Ethiopia they must have been pleased to see Um Raquba. According to volunteers and aid workers, some of the Falashas from the more remote villages thought that they had arrived in the promised land and knelt to kiss the barren soil in front of the field hospital. When they discovered that this was not Jerusalem they wept.

The camp had been established in 1976 for 2,000 Ethiopian refugees from Gondar. But by 1984 it had grown into a small township housing 20,000 people. Um Raquba was divided into two distinct sections. On a slight incline stood the 'settled' camp where there were 10,000 Christian refugees from Ethiopia, most of whom had been there for some years. Many of these veteran refugees had worked the surrounding lands in the good years before the drought and had prospered. The settled camp consisted of hundreds of *tukuls* as well as more solidly constructed buildings, such as the clinic, school and church. Half a mile away down a dirt road was the second part of the camp known as the Reception Centre, which was an area of *tukuls* and canvas tents radiating out from a simple field hospital built of wood and straw. The Reception Centre was intended for newly arrived refugees. In November 1984, before the beginning of Operation Moses, there were about

9,000 Falashas in this section of the camp. Over the previous seven or eight months, the Falashas were the only refugees to arrive in this part of Sudan in any numbers. The Falashas began arriving some six months before the greater flow of refugees from famine-struck Tigre and Eritrea, most of whom crossed into Sudan in the vicinity of Kassala.

The camp was run by the Sudan Commission for Refugees in conjunction with the Sudan Council of Churches (scc). The Commission was represented by the camp's director and the scc by two Swedish relief workers on loan from the Swedish Council of Churches. In practice, the care and management of the newly arrived refugees was in the hands of the two Swedes, Peter, the camp administrator, and Elizabeth, the camp nurse. The Commission and the scc were entirely dependent for supplies on the unhcr, which among other things was responsible for administering the un World Food Programme.

The two Swedes were evangelical Christians and, as they put it, 'vocationally missionaries'. Peter said to me: 'We are Christians, I mean committed Christians, so obviously we would like these Jews to stay with us here in the camp and perhaps in time become followers of Jesus. But they are leaving and they do have a wonderful chance to escape and get away.' He said it with a certain regret. The two Swedes were clearly devoted and caring people working in incredibly difficult circumstances. Yet their missionary orientation might have made itself obvious to the Falashas who, as a community, had been suffering at the hands of missionaries for the previous 150 years.

For the Falashas, Um Raquba hardly proved to be much of a refuge. The physical condition of most of the newcomers actually deteriorated while they were in the camp. Many of them died. Robin Townsend, a British Project Trust volunteer who was working with the Falashas in the Reception Centre from March to August 1984, told me that during this period the Falashas were dying at an average of eight every day. On one day in June, fifty died. He believes that by the end of August about 1,400 of the Falashas had perished. By November

1984, I counted about 1,600 crudely built stone cairns, which served as the final resting-place for the Falasha dead. According to the camp records, 1,939 Falashas perished between April and November 1984: 1,202 of these were under fifteen. In July 481 Falashas died and in August 397.

The Falashas believe that many of the dead were not buried in the cemetery but were disposed of hurriedly by Ethiopian and Sudanese camp workers who threw them into ditches. The Falashas complained bitterly about this and it led to many arguments in the camp. To solve the problem the Falashas mounted guard over their sick and when they died buried them very early in the morning or late at night according to their own rites. In the worst months, the Jews were so weak that five or six of them would get together to carry the corpse to the burial place, scratch out a shallow grave and pile a few stones over it. Death was such a frequent visitor to the camp that when the Falashas of Um Raquba went to Israel they still believed that any illness, even a light cold, would lead to death. An Israeli social worker told me: 'Every time one of them gets sick, the rest of the group stands around the sick bed waiting for his death. The children in the youth absorption centres do it too. They explain that they had seen their parents do this in the Sudanese camp to ensure that no one took the body and threw it onto a rubbish tip or buried it with the Christians.'

The appalling conditions in the camps led some to return to Ethiopia. In November 1984, Gary Ackerman, an American congressman, accompanied by an aide, David Feltman, visited Gondar. Feltman met one young Falasha who had returned to Ethiopia after a six-month wait in the camps and heard that 'between sixty and 200 others had walked back'. He also heard from the Falashas still in Ethiopia that 4,000 Ethiopian Jews had died on the march to Sudan and in the refugee camps. This figure is accepted by most of the Falashas I spoke to in Israel, although some put it even higher.

Why did so many of them die? In the first place there was no water supply to the Falasha part of the camp until August

1984, when an English engineer came and drilled a well. Prior to that, water was brought by donkey from the well in the settled camp and was distributed around the *tukuls* in large oil drums. The Falashas believed that they had been forced to drink tainted water while the good water was kept back for the other refugees. This was reported as fact by the BBC Television News on 4 January. It is not true, but the truth is bad enough. As one aid worker told me: 'The water situation was catastrophic. The water in the oil barrels got dirty and spread disease quicker than anything. Many of the Falashas had infectious diseases. The distribution of water was one of the most important contributory factors to the high death toll. A well should have been drilled much earlier, but in Sudan such things take time. For a sense of emergency to be generated which was acute enough to get that well built, hundreds of people had to die first.' Bad water supply plagued the other camps where the Falashas went. In Wad el Heluw, which was run by Canadian Physicians for African Refugees (CPAR), refugees were drinking badly polluted water from the river Setit (Takkaze) until a well was drilled in the summer of 1984, and in Tewawa, where there is still no water supply, water brought from Gedaref was distributed in oil drums.

Volunteers working in Um Raquba and Wad el Heluw maintain that the distribution of food was also poorly organized. The food was handed out by Christian refugees from the settled camp under the overall supervision of the Sudanese camp director and foreign aid workers. The Falashas constantly argued that they were discriminated against and did not get their fair share of food. But even if they had received their fair share, during most of 1984 there was not nearly enough food in the camp stores to go around. On a number of occasions the Falashas went for periods of seven or eight days without any food. One Falasha I met in Um Raquba told me that during the summer they had gone for three weeks without food. Aid workers confirm that for much of the period the only food in the large concrete stores consisted of oil and dried peas. Despite the drought, there was no particular shortage of food in the nearby towns and villages. While I was in Um Raquba I saw vast herds of cattle being driven past the gates of the camp: meat, grain and vegetables were for sale in the settled camp. But as the Falashas had no money, they were dependent upon what they were given.

The medical facilities in the Reception Centre were grimly inadequate. The wards consisted of rectangular grass huts open at the front. There were few blankets and during some parts of the year the nights are cold. There was very little in the way of medical equipment. For the many months that the Falashas were in the camp there was no doctor. One international organization with an office in Khartoum knew of the terrible medical conditions in the camp and was prepared to send a doctor to work there. The local authorities are reported to have refused this offer of assistance on the grounds that supplying doctors to camps was not part of that organization's brief and, in any case, would bring unwanted publicity to the Falasha question. Other voluntary organizations, such as Save the Children Fund, tried to get a doctor to Um Raquba, but the Sudan Council of Churches was reluctant to let other organizations onto 'its territory'. No doctor was sent and people carried on dying. When I visited the camp in November, the only trained medical personnel were two nurses: Elizabeth, the Swedish nurse working for the Sudan Council of Churches, and a partly trained Ethiopian nurse, himself a refugee. Between them they did everything, including complicated surgical operations for which they had received no training at all. The Sudanese director of the camp told me that in case of real emergency it would theoretically be possible to call on the facilities of the small hospital in the neighbouring town of Doka. He assured me, incredibly, that since he had been director of the camp no such emergency had arisen. The diseases that were the most prevalent in the camp were malaria, tuberculosis, hepatitis, measles, meningitis, dysentery and cholera.

Overcrowding was another of the factors that led to the spread of disease among the Falashas in Um Raquba. The reception area of the camp was not big enough for the unprecedented influx of Falashas in the first half of 1984. The situation is said to have been exacerbated by the Falashas' dislike of using canvas tents. According to a report prepared by the UNHCR, they preferred the traditional *tukul* even though it sometimes meant that fourteen or fifteen of them would be crowded into a space intended for four or five. In Wad el Heluw too, the Falashas preferred to remain in their own overcrowded quarter than to be split up and given accommodation elsewhere in the camp. They derived a sense of security from being together and were afraid of the consequences of moving to the Christian parts of the camp.

The Falashas' distrust of the outside world can be readily understood. The relationship between Christians and Jews in Ethiopia had for generations been based on fear and contempt. The situation in the camps was no different. One evening while I was in Um Raquba I sat enjoying a cup of coffee with a group of Ethiopian Christian camp workers. Not far away a group of ragged Falashas sat watching us pensively. One of the Ethiopians pointed at the group and said, 'Those people are Jews. They killed Christ.' His eyes flashed as he said it and it was clear that he held this wretched group of Falashas personally responsible for deicide. Another Ethiopian joined in: 'Some people believe that they caused the famine in Ethiopia and that is why they have been driven out by the army; they have brought disease with them to this camp and many Christians have died.' The Christians were often very fearful of the Falashas. Some of the recent Christian refugees in Um Raquba refused to go to the clinic in the Reception Centre as there were always Falashas in the vicinity. Aid workers in the camp frequently heard rumours that the Falashas eat people, particularly Christians, and cause women to have miscarriages. Falashas who were particularly active or energetic were believed to have the evil eye: a number were pointed out to me, rather discreetly, by other refugees. Falashas believed to have the evil eye were attacked in the camps and from more than one source I heard the terrible story of a young Falasha who, only a mile from the Sudanese border and what he believed to be safety, was torn apart by a group of Ethiopian refugees who feared that he had the evil eye. Not surprisingly, the Falashas in most circumstances tried to pass themselves off as Christians. In view of the fierce animosity directed against them by the other Ethiopians, the Falashas' claim that they were discriminated against by the Christian camp workers who distributed the food may well be correct.

The fundamental problem of the Falashas in Sudan was that they were completely unused to the conditions that they encountered. A highland people, they were suddenly faced with the searing heat of the Sudanese plains and quickly fell prey to lowland diseases such as malaria. But they were ill-equipped for camp life for other reasons. All the aid workers I spoke to stressed that the Falashas were the most vulnerable group within the camps because they were reluctant to seek help from outside. They exhibited a profound distrust of aid workers and of the other refugees. Whereas the Christian refugees in camps like Wad el Heluw would soon find out what was available to them and would wait outside the clinic and demand attention, the Falashas would stick to their own quarter and were unwilling even to take their children for supplementary feeding when it was available. As one volunteer who had been working as a health visitor in Wad el Heluw put it: 'They only accepted help when it was pushed on them. They seemed sad, silent people, closed to the outside world. Unlike the Christians, they hardly communicated with us at all.'

Another reason for the Falashas' timidity is perhaps that they were reluctant to draw any attention to themselves for fear that the secret operations that were slowly taking them to Israel should be discovered. The Falasha envoys who came from Gedaref to Um Raquba every few days impressed upon the Falashas the need for absolute discretion and secrecy. Their fate lay in the hands of their rescuers and all they could do was to wait patiently. When weeks and months passed and still they had not been taken to Israel they became very frustrated.

One Falasha decided to leave the camp on his own. He walked out into the desert and the next day was found by an army patrol. Rather than return with them to Um Raquba, he slashed his wrists in front of them. An official of the UNHCR, quoted in the *Sunday Times*, said that he had come across a group of 200 Falashas waiting on a dirt road outside Gedaref. They had left their camp and were waiting for a courier to take them to Israel. While the official was looking at the group one of the Falashas committed suicide. Expecting immediate redemption at the end of their punishing trek and being forced to wait in terrible circumstances for the realization of their messianic dreams, they became more and more desperate. In this sense they were worse off than the other Ethiopian refugees, who had walked into Sudan with no greater expectation than that they might find something to eat. The Falashas' frustrations were transformed into suspicion of everything around them.

They were sometimes suspicious of those who were trying to help them leave the camps. Joshua told me: 'Sometimes when we came to take them from the camps in trucks they were reluctant to leave. They said that we were going to take them away and kill them. No one on the outside had ever shown kindness to some of these people. They could not understand why *we* should want to help them. I remember one young man was particularly vehement about being taken from the camp. I saw him a couple of days later getting on to one of the planes in Khartoum and I asked him: "Do you still think we are trying to kill you?" He gave me a look of such pure and profound gratitude that I shall not forget it for the rest of my life.'

The Falashas' own dietary regulations contributed to their plight in Um Raquba and elsewhere. Throughout 1984 the only cooking oil which was available in the camp was Norwegian whale fat, which the Falashas would not use because it is not kosher. The Falashas refused to compromise their religious laws even when they were starving. They were suspicious of all foods with which they were unfamiliar, perhaps because they were not sure if they were 'permitted' or not.

Even when they arrived in Israel there were Falasha women who would only eat bread for fear that other foods were not kosher. But they were slow to adapt even to 'permitted' food: there was, for instance, no *teff* and many of them did not know what to do with the wheat and sorghum which were sometimes available. They would sell the grain and whale fat they had been given to the refugees in the settled camp for much less than their market value and buy small quantities of coffee, sugar and vegetable oil. The dried peas, which were often available in some quantities, they insisted on frying and eating one by one like peanuts. Coffee, which they had known in Ethiopia, they would drink several times a day. An insulated, highland people, they were tragically slow to adapt to their new environment.

The Falashas were also suspicious about the medical arrangements in the camps and at some point conceived the notion that the Ethiopian medical auxiliaries were trying to poison them. This belief arose because when they had first arrived at the camp they had been given injections against the diseases that they already had, such as malaria or hepatitis. At the same time they were all suffering from severe dehydration, but the Falashas were reluctant to eat the salt tablets which were distributed and, as a result, many of them died. But the deaths from dehydration were attributed by the Falashas to the injections. Subsequently, many of the Falashas and particularly those from the more remote villages were very suspicious of the camp clinic. They had seen people die, apparently as a result of having medical treatment, and they preferred, in some cases, to resort to their own traditional cures. They placed particular reliance on blood-letting. The 'bad blood' was let off just above the elbow or on the side of the face above the eyebrow. They often hid their sick and particularly their children so that the health visitors would not be able to take them to the clinic.

As the deaths continued the Falashas in Um Raquba became even more desperate. At one point their people were dying at the rate of fifteen to twenty a day and nothing, it seemed, could be done to prevent it. The elders of the camp got together and after much discussion decided on a course of action. Half a mile away, between the Falasha camp and the cemetery, stood a rugged hill on the summit of which an Ethiopian Muslim 'wizard' had constructed an elaborate stone-built compound. Christians and Muslims from the adjoining Ethiopian camp visited the wizard and against a small payment received cures and advice on personal matters. The Falasha elders visited him and were advised to sacrifice two cows, one red, one black, and a white goat. Money was collected throughout the community and the beasts were purchased from a neighbouring village and were sacrificed according to Falasha custom.

One Falasha who had been in the camp told me: 'It was like what happened to the Israelites in Egypt before they went to the Land of Israel. They suffered many plagues before they were delivered. It purified the people for the Holy Land.' The young man seemed uneasy with this explanation.

By the late summer of 1984, accounts started to appear in the press throughout the world of the high death toll among the Falashas in east Sudan. On 11 September, the French *Libération* reported that ten per cent of the Falashas who had left their homes had died *en route*. The next day, *Figaro*, quoting UNHCR sources in Geneva, put out that several hundred Jews had died in Um Raquba after their arrival in Sudan. A few days later the Toronto *Globe and Mail* and the *International Herald Tribune* carried the story that 'at least 1,300 black Ethiopian Jews, mostly children, have died in refugee camps'. The Israeli authorities were given a dramatic eye-witness account of the plight of the Falashas in the camps by Henry Gold, a young Canadian Jew who had been working for Canadian Physicians for African Refugees.

CPAR, a broadly based aid organization, was running Wad el Heluw refugee camp until it was asked to leave the Sudan in August 1984. The organization was specifically involved in helping the Falashas and at least one of its workers was subsequently to visit Falasha groups in Ethiopa. All their workers were concerned for the Falashas. Gold established a

considerable reputation among the Falashas who knew that he
viewed their predicament sympathetically and would offer
what practical help he could. After the premature disclosure
of Operation Moses, *The Times* (7 January 1985) reported
that when the Falashas had first arrived in Sudan 'many
were told to ask for a "Mr Gold", believed to have been a
code-name used during the operation'. 'Gold' was not a
code-name nor was Gold involved in the operation except in
the most minor way. The chief reason for CPAR's expulsion
from the country was that it was making its interest in the
Falashas too obvious and getting in the way of the operation
which was being organized and conducted in quite different
quarters.

When he arrived in Jerusalem, Gold reported that

Refugees who arrive in the camps healthy are reduced to human
skeletons after three months, almost to the state of concentration
camp victims.... All I know is that I now understand for the first
time why the people who escaped from concentration camps, but
couldn't get anyone to believe what was happening, committed suicide. A major disaster is happening to all the refugees, not just the
Jews ... if world Jewry doesn't act we can add another destroyed
community to the Diaspora Museum exhibits of fifty-two destroyed
Jewish historical communities.... I truly believe that if relatively
swift action is not forthcoming this could end in another terribly sad
chapter for our people.

Gold explained that the unprecedented arrival of such a
large number of Falashas in one place had thrown local
officials into confusion. He claimed in addition that the
UNHCR had adopted a policy of deliberately maintaining the
camps at a minimal nutritional level for fear of encouraging
more refugees to flood over the border from Ethiopia. This
suggestion had no justification.

Perhaps the main reason for the high death toll among the
Falashas was the fact that the camp at Um Raquba was
not prepared for such a large influx of people and that the
organizations involved were pitifully slow to react. According

to the camp figures, the Falashas came at the following rate: March – 1,113; April – 2,523; May – 2,125; June – 1,627; July – 2,500; August – 2,012. They usually arrived in groups of around fifty a day, although during May 1,000 arrived in just two days. The camp was not able to cope.

The UNHCR bears some of the responsibility for what happened. Quite clearly the camps were badly run, there was not enough food or water and the medical provisions were minimal. Also, during the first months of 1984, the UNHCR channels of communication seem to have broken down. The main concentration of Falashas, at Um Raquba, was visited on a regular basis by a UNHCR official, Nicholas Swingwa, who knew of the conditions prevalent in the camp. He reported to Peter Parr, the director of the Gedaref sub-office of UNHCR, which is where the information seems to have stopped. When Nicholas Morris, the Khartoum director of UNHCR, went on leave in June, he seemed to a former colleague of his to be unaware of the crisis. A number of sources have indicated that the information stopped in the Gedaref sub-office and was not transmitted. Parr has since been replaced. UNHCR has admitted that it was 'slow in appreciating how serious the conditions were', but claims that the Sudan Council of Churches, who were running the camp for the Sudan Commission for Refugees, failed to report the deaths. Clearly, as the UNHCR sent their own officials to inspect the camp, this was hardly necessary.

It has been argued that the Mossad could have stopped the exodus in the spring of 1984 when it became clear that the camps were unable to cope with the high number of refugees. This would have been impossible. By 1984 the process of Falasha emigration had snowballed and become a spontaneous movement of people from hundreds of different villages. At short notice nothing could be done to stop it.

When Henry Gold arrived in Jerusalem, the Israelis knew full well what was going on in the camps from Mossad and AAEJ sources and had been negotiating with increasing desperation for some months to solve the problem. In response to Gold's report the Jewish Agency declined absolutely to comment, believing that any spotlight on the Falashas would be dangerous. The Foreign Office replied that Israel's policy was 'to get the Falasha home to Israel and that policy is being pursued in every possible way today as well'.

CHAPTER EIGHT

Operation Moses

The unprecedented numbers of Falashas migrating from Ethiopia to Sudan in the early months of 1984 and the rising death toll in the refugee camps created a grave problem both for the Israeli and for the Sudanese authorities. The Israeli government was committed to bringing the Falashas to Israel, but they were dying in the camps of eastern Sudan faster than they could be got out. A discreet and gradual operation was no longer enough. For their part, the Sudanese realized that such a large influx of Falashas changed the scope of the operation and risked attention being focused on their presence in Sudan and their passage to Israel.

From the Sudanese point of view, the Falasha problem had to be contained. It was Numeiri's normal practice to place trusted political appointees in key military and other sensitive posts. These were frequently drawn from the 47,000-strong *AmnulDawla*. It was decided to remove the officials in charge of the camps where the Jews were and to substitute men whose discretion could be relied upon. In Um Raquba, Said al-Hanifi, the camp director, was arrested and imprisoned on charges of being a communist and replaced by Osman el-Zaki, a Khartoum civil servant with security connections. In Wad el Heluw, Abu Rahil, an agent of the *AmnulDawla*, was given control of the camp. Security police were brought in to patrol the Falasha areas of the camps. The Canadian Physicians for African Refugees, who were showing too keen an interest in the Falashas, were cautioned and finally ordered out of Sudan. The United States gave what help they could. In September the State Department cancelled a contract with Sudanaid, the relief arm of the Catholic Bishops' Conference, which ran a 'work-generating' project in Tewawa, the marshalling point for the projected exodus. Relief workers say that the *Amnul-Dawla* wanted the two Sudanaid workers who had been working in Tewawa out of the way because they already knew far too much.

At the same time the Sudanese tried to stem the flood of Falashas crossing the border. The army was given the task of sealing the frontier areas as best it could and the Falasha couriers were instructed not to bring any more Jews across. For a period of about three weeks in May and June this initiative was successful and no Falashas at all arrived at the reception centres. The camp directors were told to prevent unofficial movements out of the camps. One group of about thirty Falashas who had left Wad el Heluw were caught by army units and taken on to the more inaccessible Um Raquba camp. Throughout the year, attempts were made to concentrate the Falashas in Um Raquba and every effort was made to prevent them from leaving the camp. Information about the Falashas was controlled and monitored by the *AmnulDawla*. In the Falasha camps working volunteers were told to report directly to the camp directors on Falasha movements and numbers.

Although the Sudanese had not been unco-operative in facilitating the operation thus far, they now refused to allow the Israelis to undertake any large-scale action to rescue the Falashas from the camps. The political risks, it was argued, were simply too great. The Israelis asked the American government to apply some pressure on Sudan and when President Reagan's roving ambassador, General Vernon Walters, visited Khartoum in the spring, he is said to have included the plight of the Falashas in his discussions with the Sudanese President. Numeiri refused to give any ground and Walters reported back to Washington that Numeiri was becoming increasingly difficult to deal with on this and other issues.

In July, a number of secret cabinet meetings were held in Jerusalem on the urgent need to rescue the Falashas from the terrible conditions of the camps. Various options were reportedly considered, but it was decided that without Sudanese

co-operation very little could be done. In September, Yitzhak
Shamir, the Deputy Prime Minister in the Israeli coalition
government, visited Washington for routine talks with George
Shultz, the American Secretary of State. By now it was known
that the situation of the Falashas was desperate. Presenting
the Israeli case, Shamir argued that the huge population
movements in Sudan and Ethiopia caused by the drought and
the famine would enable the Falashas to be extricated from
the country without anyone being any the wiser. Movements
of refugees through Khartoum Airport were already a commonplace and no one would be able to tell a Falasha from
any other Ethiopian refugee. The famine provided the perfect
cover. Shultz agreed to bring American pressure to bear on
Numeiri.

The United States had been involved in the Falasha emigration through Sudan for some time. American Jewry has
formidable lobbying power in Washington and for years the
Falasha question had been raised by Jewish Falasha activists
and Jewish organizations generally. In July 1983, the *Congres-
sional Record* reported that it was

resolved by the United States Senate (the House of Representatives
concurring) that it is the sense of the Congress that the President
should:

(1) express to relevant foreign governments the United States concern for the welfare of the Ethiopian Jews, in particular their
right to emigrate;
(2) seek ways to assist Ethiopian Jews through every available
means so that they may be able to emigrate freely.

A number of Jews in key positions in Washington made it
their business to promote the interests of the Falashas, and a
few senators and congressmen had been very active on this
issue. Howard Wolpe, chairman of the House of Representatives' sub-committee on African affairs, made an unpublicized
visit to the Falasha areas of Gondar in 1983 and is said to
have played an active role in facilitating the emigration of the

Falashas since his return. In September 1984, as a result of
pressure from within Washington, the US Congress discussed
the Falasha affair for no less than six days!

The American official within Sudan most responsible for
implementing American policy on the Falashas was Jerry
Weaver, who officially had the position of refugee co-ordinator
at the Khartoum US embassy. Described by one Khartoum-
based diplomat as 'something of an adventurer', Weaver en-
joyed close links with the head of the *AmnulDawla*, Omar al-
Tayeb, as well as with the various organizations concerned
with refugee welfare. He was thus well placed to co-ordinate
action between the United States and the various concerned
parties. From the spring of 1984, Weaver kept a close eye on
the Falashas. He visited Um Raquba twice, in April and July,
on one occasion accompanied by Peter Parr. He visited Wad
el Heluw even more frequently and was fully aware of the
deteriorating condition of the camp. It can be assumed that
Weaver's reports to Washington underlined the need for
action. Before and during the phase of the airlift, working
alongside Joshua, Weaver was one of the key men in the
operation. He, more than anyone else in Sudan, represented
Israeli interests regarding the Falashas to the *AmmulDawla*.
Officials in the Sudan Commission for Refugees, aware of
Weaver's connections with the operation, complained that the
US embassy always used 'aid' very politically and that the
Falasha affair was just another instance of it.

If the United States chose to apply real pressure to Numeiri
on any issue, there was very little he could do but comply.
Sudan was a sadly impotent state. For years there had been
sporadic conditions of drought in Sudan and in the surrounding countries. Once hailed as the future bread-basket of the
Arab world, it now needed to import over a million tons of
cereal a year just to feed its own population. Hundreds of
thousands of Sudanese were starving. But Sudan had a vast
refugee population as well. By August 1984 there were 490,000
Ethiopians in eastern Sudan and hundreds of thousands of
victims of the drought were converging on the country from
Eritrea and Tigre. On both counts Sudan could not exist

without foreign aid and the United States was by far the most important donor: eighty per cent of the budget of the UNHCR came from the United States government and seventy-five per cent of Sudan's food shortfall was provided by the USA.

Some of the problems of Sudan could no doubt be attributed to Numeiri's Islamization programme first introduced in the autumn of 1983. Economically the application of Islamic law (*Sharia*) was a disaster: conventional income tax was replaced by the *zakat* – the Islamic poor-rate – which is levied on capital at a modest two and a half per cent. Banking was affected similarly. Sudan badly needed to borrow money, but in the circumstances (and until Sudan repaid the $100 million it owed the International Monetary Fund) there were few countries or institutions that were prepared to oblige. Most significantly, the application of *Sharia* law and the acceleration of Islamization had the effect of sharpening and prolonging the military conflict between the government and the Sudanese People's Liberation Movement in the non-Muslim south. By the summer of 1984 government forces had little control in the south outside the main towns. The escalating war in the area further depleted the state's pitifully inadequate coffers.

The fact that Ethiopia and Libya had been training and supplying the southern rebels led to a dramatic worsening of relations between Sudan and these two states. To the north, Egypt was increasingly disenchanted with Numeiri and there were several members of Mubarak's government who regarded the Sudanese leader as a 'liability'. Numeiri's support in the rest of the Arab world had dwindled despite his tactical jump onto the Islamic bandwagon. Almost completely isolated anyway, without American military and financial aid, Numeiri would have been lost.

Obviously, in any negotiations with Sudan, the United States held all the cards. But despite the frailty of his position, Numeiri put up a long, hard fight. His chief fear was that his political enemies, the Muslim Brothers, whom he openly called the Brothers of Satan, would discover his secret dealings and make political capital out of them. In addition, his standing in the Arab world would inevitably suffer if the story came out. According to one highly placed Jerusalem source: 'Numeiri was very difficult to persuade. The negotiations were very tough, inconclusive and difficult. They also went on for a long time.'

In the middle of 1984, Numeiri was in a difficult position from every point of view. His chief concern had become the complete control of the internal media, the tightening of state security and manœuvring for increased foreign aid. Despite the obvious dangers inherent in helping the United States and Israel get the black Jews out of his country, it became apparent to him that the risks could be offset by considerable financial gain.

Reports in the press after the premature cancellation of the airlift suggested that the Sudanese were persuaded to co-operate by 'hard cash – about $60 million raised by Jewish benefactors in the United States'. Other reports suggested that Israel had supplied Sudan with arms in exchange for which Numeiri had agreed to turn a blind eye to the airlift. Neither Jewish money nor Israeli arms were involved. The carrot was increased American aid. In the 1984 fiscal year Sudan received $197·4 million, of which $46·5 million was in military assistance. For the 1985 fiscal year the United States had guaranteed $250 million. According to some reports the operation had to be postponed until the American Congress passed the new allocation in October 1984.

As the negotiations dragged on, the Israelis had to find a way of mounting an operation which would take into account the numerous restrictions imposed by the Sudanese. The easiest and cheapest way of moving 10,000 people quickly from eastern Sudan to Israel is by sea via Port Sudan. Numeiri found this suggestion politically unacceptable because it involved a direct journey from Sudan to Israel, and such a movement of people would have been highly visible within Sudan. There were logistical reasons, too, for not using the sea route: much of the available transport in Sudan was required to transfer food to the refugee areas where people were dying of starvation. There was also a critical shortage of petrol within the country. The idea of a mass airlift was also rejected on political grounds as was the use of Israeli civil or military aircraft. The Sudanese were not, however, opposed to using civil airlines out of Khartoum's International Airport. After all, the Falashas had been travelling out of Sudan in small groups for the previous four years without the world being any the wiser. With the use of specially chartered planes, the Sudanese felt there was a good chance the operation could go undetected.

The Israelis had the task of finding a co-operative civilian airline, which could fly the Falashas to a third country and then on to Israel without arousing too much suspicion either within Sudan or in the transit country. As the Sudanese would only permit one flight a day for reasons of discretion, a large airline was not necessary. What was required was a sympathetic company whose presence in Sudan would attract no particular attention. Someone had the inspired idea of enlisting the support of Georges Gutelman.

Gutelman, an orthodox Belgian Jew, was the fifty-one-year-old director of a Belgian charter company called Trans European Airways (TEA). The company, which boasted six Boeing 737s, one Airbus A300, as well as a number of Boeing 707s, was known to have a lot of business with the American forces in Europe. Gutelman also had close business links with Israel, particularly in the arms business, and had recently been trying to sell American radar-jamming devices, refined and adapted by Israel during the Lebanese war, to the Belgian air force for use in its F16 aircraft. Gutelman also held the contract from the Belgian air force to overhaul the F16 navigation systems. A man with such interests could be relied upon not to be indiscreet. But there were two things about Gutelman that made him the perfect choice for Operation Moses. He was a friend of Israel and his airline had close links with Sudan. For years TEA had been flying Muslim pilgrims from Sudan and other North African countries to Mecca. The sight of TEA planes flying in and out of Khartoum would surprise no one.

Gutelman was not hard to persuade. He accepted the possibility that he might lose his lucrative Arab contracts. His reward, as he saw it, was that he would be able to play a role in the redemption of the Jewish people. Explaining his decision, Gutelman is reported to have quoted the famous line of Maimonides: 'There is no greater obligation than the redemption of captives.'

In September 1984, Gutelman was asked to make the necessary arrangements for the airlift. There were a number of difficulties to be overcome. It would clearly be impossible to airlift thousands of refugees to Israel via a third country without that country knowing something about it. The best cover for the operation would be for TEA to transit its own airport in Brussels. This, however, could implicate the Belgian government, which would hardly agree to a scheme that might damage Belgium's relations with Ethiopia as well as the Arab world.

Gutelman soon found a way around the difficulty. He approached Jean Gol, the Belgian Minister of Justice and Vice-Premier, who was an old friend of his and also a fellow Jew. As the minister responsible for the Belgian Security Service, Gol was the one man in Belgium who would need to be informed. Persuaded that the operation could be carried off in secrecy, Gol secured the approval of his Prime Minister, Wilfried Martens, and promised Gutelman and the Israelis that he would co-operate. Within the Belgian government access to the information was on a 'need to know' basis. When the news of the airlift was leaked in January 1985, Belga, the Belgian news agency, announced that even the Belgian Ministry of Foreign Affairs had been unaware of what was going on as they 'had not been required to provide any specific authorization'.

The Americans presented the suggestion that TEA be used for the operation and the Sudan government gave its consent. Ten thousand Falashas could be flown out of Khartoum Airport to Israel via an airport in a third country at the rate of one planeload a day.

On their side, the Sudanese continued to tighten up their security arrangements. More security police were dispatched to the camps where the Falashas were. Um Raquba was to be sealed off from the outside world. The other camps were to be barred to visitors. In October, Ahmad Abdul Rahman, the Sudan Commissioner for Refugees, was fired on the pretext that, in defiance of *Sharia*, he had been drinking hard liquor. According to Sudanese officials I spoke to in Khartoum, Abdul Rahman had simply been asking too many questions.

More Israeli agents, most of them Israeli Falashas, were brought into Sudan to prepare the ground. Although most of the Falashas were in Um Raquba, Tewawa and Wad el Heluw camps, there were pockets of Falashas living outside the camps, in Gedaref and its miserable suburbs, and there were groups of Falashas from Tigre who had got no further than the huge refugee complexes in the vicinity of Kassala. They all had to be told that rescue was imminent and brought to one of the centres near Gedaref. This was no easy task. The Falashas in all the camps had been trying to pass themselves off as Christians and, where there were few of them, they were often accepted as such. This meant that they were difficult to find. According to some reports, at the height of the operation there were eighty 'spotters' in Sudan locating Falashas and getting them ready to be transported to Israel.

In October, according to later reports in the *Los Angeles Times*, a Khartoum-based diplomat went to Geneva, where he met with Israeli Mossad and Jewish Agency officials. Over the next month one million dollars passed through his hands. He was commissioned to buy four buses, five long-range vehicles for visiting the outlying camps, and 500 metric tons of fuel at the cost of $175,000. Further safe-houses were bought or rented in Gedaref and Khartoum. One aspect of the agreement with the *AmnulDawla* was that after the operation they would inherit the vehicles that were bought to ferry the Jews to Khartoum.

On 21 November Operation Moses started. Hundreds of Falashas had been brought or had made their own way to Tewawa, on the outskirts of Gedaref which was only a few minutes' drive from the main Gedaref–Khartoum road. Every night after dark, the four recently purchased buses accompanied by security police took the refugees from Gedaref to Khartoum, where they were accommodated in safe-houses. The following night they were driven to the closely guarded entrance to the military part of Khartoum Airport and were driven straight up to the waiting TEA plane, which was standing at the end of a runway in a disused part of the airport. From the moment the Falashas left Tewawa to the time they stepped onto the plane that would take them to Israel, they were accompanied and supervised by Sudanese security agents and Falasha agents working for the Mossad. Of the Westerners co-operating with the airlift, Jerry Weaver was the only one allowed anywhere near the Belgian planes. Every conceivable precaution was taken to safeguard the secrecy of the operation.

TEA conducted itself with great discretion throughout the operation. The Belgian TEA crews were accommodated in Khartoum in the Friendship Palace Hotel situated on the far side of the Blue Nile some way from Khartoum's busy centre. They were very uncommunicative about what they were doing. Gutelman himself kept a very low profile throughout the period of the airlift and even after the interruption of the airlift gave instructions to his staff to reveal neither details of the company's interests or movements, nor of the role it had played in the operation. The success of Operation Moses is due in no small part to the discipline and organization of the 200 people working within his organization at Zaventen International Airport at Brussels. His entire workforce was aware of the origins and destination of the human cargo that was being smuggled every night through Belgium. No one said a word.

Between the last week of November 1984 and the first week of January 1985, Boeing 707s of the TEA fleet flew, in all, thirty-five flights between Khartoum and Tel Aviv. There were no flights on Saturdays: the Falashas would have been horrified at the thought of desecrating the Sabbath. The planes overflew Egypt on the way to Brussels where, at around midnight, they landed for a two-hour stopover for refuelling and other services. The aircraft were officially listed simply as 'charter flights in transit', a cheerful designation which contrasts harshly with the scenes of human misery which attended the twelve-hour flights. To minimize risk of discovery at Zaventen Airport, the planes stayed at the end of the runway and at no time approached the terminal. The doctors and nurses who accompanied every flight were kept busy. As a matter of policy and of principle, the Mossad had ensured that those who were brought out first were those least able to fend for themselves: the old, the sick and the orphaned. Some died and others were born in the air on the way to Israel. There was always the fear that the flights would have to be cancelled. If some Falashas had to be left behind to await a further operation, it should be those that had the best chance of surviving in the crowded refugee camps. The arrival of one planeload of Falashas at Ben-Gurion Airport was described by the Israel Defence Force's radio station:

First off the plane were two children who were attached to transfusion tubes. They were put into ambulances with their parents. The Ethiopians arrived destitute. At first they were very frightened, but when they realized that they had arrived in the Holy Land, they asked the direction of Jerusalem and knelt on the runway, kissing the ground, praying towards the Holy City. Almost all the children who got off the plane were barefoot. Some were naked except for a T-shirt. The only possessions that some brought with them were yellow water carriers.

Despite the special security arrangements made by the *Amnul-Dawla*, at the beginning of December I was able to get through to Um Raquba, where the Falashas were preparing themselves to leave for Israel. I travelled on refugee trucks, which were not stopped by the security guards on the outskirts of Gedaref. I was lucky. On 10 December, a car carrying some aid workers, a visiting Canadian parliamentarian and a British photographer was stopped near Tewawa by the *AmnulDawla*. The car had been following four buses taking Falashas to Khartoum and, it is alleged, the photographer was seen trying to get a picture of the buses. The two aid workers, Nick Miscione, an American, and Gabriel Daniels, an Ethiopian living in the United States, both of whom were working for Sudanaid, were arrested and later expelled from the country. The Canadian and the British photographer were held under house arrest in Gedaref for thirty hours and then encouraged to leave the area.

Security measures of this sort ensured that the operation proceeded smoothly. The airlift was an extraordinarily well-guarded secret in Sudan although, unknown to the Sudanese, the secret was not being as well-kept elsewhere.

By the summer of 1984 the exodus from Ethiopia was common knowledge at least among Jewish groups in the United States. In its Summer 1984 issue, *Reform Judaism* reported that

hundreds [of Falashas] are currently leaving via a dangerous and illegal eight-day walk into neighbouring countries, where they wait in refugee villages for covert Israeli military rescue. Israel has more than doubled its rescue efforts recently and is now bringing out more than 300 Jews each month. Currently there are more than 5,400 Ethiopian Jews living in Israel.

The AAEJ took the full credit for this as for every other initiative. In the Autumn 1984 issue of its magazine *Release*, the organization claimed that

In recent months the AAEJ has rescued and brought to Israel over ONE HUNDRED Ethiopian Jews, most of whom had been in refugee camps for three years. These new immigrants are mostly women, small children and elders.... The recent AAEJ successes have stimulated the Israelis to accelerate their Falasha rescue programme which for the past year was nearly at a standstill.

Throughout the summer and the autumn the Israeli government maintained its policy of silence. From the very beginnings of the operation in 1980, this had required a great deal of restraint on the part of the politicians concerned. The frequent accusations of racism from within Israel and from abroad were charges to which Israeli governments had been particularly sensitive since the infamous 1974 UN resolution equating Zionism with racism. Even at the height of Operation Moses, when hundreds of Ethiopian Jews were secretly arriving in Israel every day, there was biting criticism of the government from within Israel. On one occasion in December, the Foreign Minister was pressed in the Knesset to explain what Israel was doing for the Falashas in view of the famine, which was increasingly beginning to command media attention. Not to be drawn, the Minister replied baldly: 'We have sent them medicine.' This generated a hostile response throughout the country, which was expressed by one of the Hebrew papers.

In the meantime thousands of Ethiopian Jews are rotting while they wait for Israel to come to their aid. Is it impossible to give them the same help as was offered to the North African Jews in the past? Is it really such a big problem? When we really wanted to, we managed to bring the Jews out of Egypt and the Yemen in much more difficult circumstances.

Despite the provocation, the government said nothing.

The criticisms of the AAEJ and the CAEJ continued until the end of 1984. On 15 November, a few days before the beginning of Operation Moses, the opening plenary session of the General Assembly of the Council of Jewish Federations was broken up by forty Falasha activists led by Jacobivici, who demanded to be allowed to speak. Holding an Ethiopian child in his arms, Jacobivici sat on the floor with his group and demanded one minute's silence for the 2,000 Jews 'who had died during the famine' and who could have been saved had Israel wished it. An article by Jacobivici, which appeared in the *New York Times* at about the same time, charged: 'Ethiopian Jews die, Israel fiddles.' The stupidity of such accusations was soon to bear bitter fruit.

The success of Operation Moses was conditional upon secrecy. Sudan could not be seen to be helping Jews, even starving black Jews from Ethiopia, because of her public position *vis à vis* the Arab–Israeli conflict and the risk of offending the more extreme members of the Arab League, such as Libya's Gadaffi and Syria's Assad as well as more moderate

rulers. In addition to these foreign policy considerations, there
were also sound internal reasons why the secret should never
be allowed to emerge. Numeiri was held in scant esteem by
the Muslim Brotherhood and the other fundamentalist groups
whose opinions he pretended to share, and any scandal impli-
cating him in direct collaboration with Israel could have been
dangerous and even fatal for his regime. In addition, there
were many Sudanese of moderate political and religious views
who would have been deeply shocked by the thought of having dealings with the Zionist enemy.

The great fear throughout the period of the airlift was that
premature publicity would force Numeiri to bring it to an
end. Shortly after my arrival in Khartoum towards the end of
November 1984, I had met Joshua for a non-alcoholic drink
at a bar overlooking the Blue Nile, a few yards from where,
twelve months before, millions of dollars worth of liquor had
been poured into the river at the onset of Numeiri's policy of
Islamization. Looking around him anxiously, Joshua said:
'This whole operation can work. It is possible. But everything
depends upon secrecy. All the sensitive areas have been sealed
off by the State Security, but if newspaper-men get into
Gedaref, we are lost. Everybody knows what is happening
there. The big worry at the moment is that Teddy Kennedy is
planning to spend Christmas in Gedaref. Can you imagine?
If his press retinue trips over the Falashas, the whole thing is
finished.'

The worry, had he known it, was far away from Khartoum.
On 15 November, a few days before the airlift started, Leon
Dulzin, the chairman of the Jewish Agency, was addressing a
session of the Council of Jewish Federations in Toronto, the
same conference whose opening session had been disrupted by
the Falasha activists. Stung, no doubt, by the memory of their
taunts, Dulzin proclaimed: 'One of the ancient tribes of Israel
is due to return to its homeland', and later in his speech:
'When the true story of the Jews of Ethiopia is told, we will
take pride in what we have already achieved in this most
difficult and complex rescue operation.' Dulzin's hopelessly
indiscreet remarks were included in a press release sent out

from the New York office of the World Zionist Organization (wzo). According to an official of the wzo (quoted in the Long Island *Jewish World*), Dulzin was given the opportunity to stop the press release but decided against doing so on the grounds that giving out some information was imperative to the United Jewish Appeal campaign. The fundamental problem was that the Jewish Agency, which depends upon voluntary subscriptions, had decided to raise the money for the absorption of the Falashas while the operation was still under way.

There were two reasons for this. In the first place it was considered that once the Ethiopian Jews got to Israel, the appeal for funds would lose its edge. This was because it had been decided to run the campaign as an appeal for funds, not to help in absorption, but rather to save lives. Operation Moses was being compared to saving Jews from Auschwitz, while Jewish newspapers in the United States and Canada carried advertisements proclaiming: 'For each $6,000 one Jewish life will be saved.' By its nature, such a campaign had to be conducted *before* the Falashas had been saved. A further factor, it has been said, was that 'fund-raisers understood that their best chance to raise funds was in the days and weeks before 31 December, when most tax deductible donations are made' (*Jewish World*). The campaign was a massive one: appeals for Operation Moses were made in almost every synagogue in the United States in the last two months of 1984. Discretion went by the board. At one Friday evening service at the Temple Valley synagogue in north Los Angeles, for instance, it was revealed that Israel was airlifting 300 Jews a day from Sudan.

Striking while the iron is hot is a normal stratagem in fund-raising. Whether it was justifiable on this occasion, given the great risks, is doubtful, but at least one can understand the motivation. The total annual budget for the Agency is $404 million, of which only $29 million comes from the Israeli government. The Agency would have been hard pressed to find more money from within Israel, whose economy is in dire straits as a result of a foreign debt of $22 billion and inflation

running at an annual 475 per cent. The predicted cost of
settling the Falashas was huge – about $25,000 per immigrant.
The money had to come from somewhere and the only Jewish
community in the world which could raise the required sums
was in the United States. At the same time, there are many
Israeli and Jewish causes competing for American Jewry's
money. Who knew what new crisis might not blow up in
Israel or elsewhere and divert funds needed for settling the
Falashas? This is the Agency's argument. But there are many
in Israel who claim that the Agency could have used its standing funds and made economies elsewhere.

The press release occasioned by Dulzin's dramatic words
was picked up by the New York *Jewish Week* on 23 November.
The headline 'Reveal Plan for the Rescue of the Falashas' was
followed by the explicit statement: 'A dramatic mass rescue of
thousands of Ethiopian Jews and their transfer to Israel is
scheduled to begin soon after 1 January.' On 6 December, the
Washington *Jewish Week* gave even more details: 'The rescue
of a substantial number of Ethiopian Jews has begun ... an
operation far more systematic than previous efforts is under
way.' On 11 December the story reached the general public
when the *New York Times* ran a front-page article which revealed that a mass airlift was in progress. Even more emerged
the following day in the *Boston Globe*. 'The United States', it
reported, 'acted as intermediary in getting Sudanese officials
and Israeli agents together to set up the complex logistics for
the humanitarian mission.' Pertinently, an American official
was quoted: 'We've got to get them out as quickly as possible
before it comes to public attention and the whole thing col-
lapses.' The story helped to ensure that it *did* come to public
attention when it was wired to every serious media outlet in
the world. The three most delicate aspects of the operation
had all been mentioned: the numbers involved, the co-operation of Sudan and the United States with Israel, and the
escape route.

For no good reason, the story died. In Belgium, where news-
men knew what was going on, not a word was written. Israeli
diplomats and American State Department officials managed

to get Jewish newspapers to leave the story alone. In Israel, the newspapers kept quiet. In Sudan, the revelations in the *New York Times* had not caused too much of a stir because the impression had been given that the airlift had been conducted out of Ethiopia. The *Boston Globe* report made no particular impact and was probably missed by the Sudanese authorities. The airlift was not interrupted and the men on the ground in Sudan felt that the crisis had passed. Their attention turned again to the Kennedy visit. On Christmas Eve, Kennedy landed not in Gedaref but further north in Kassala, a Sudanese town close to the Ethiopian border from which he was able to visit some of the huge refugee camps housing hundreds of thousands of recent refugees from Tigre and Eritrea. In the intense media coverage of the visit there was no mention of the Falashas. The Jews helping to co-ordinate the airlift were beginning to feel that with luck the operation would be a total success and that every last Falasha could be airlifted out of Sudan. By the end of December it was clear that with two more weeks their job would be over. They were wrong.

The revelations that brought the operation to an end were sparked off by an entirely innocuous article on page six of an obscure Hebrew periodical *Nekuda* (Point) enjoying a minuscule circulation among West Bank settlers. Yehuda Dominitz, at this time the Director General of the Jewish Agency, was asked how many Ethiopian Jews had emigrated to Israel in the previous year. He replied firmly: 'I am not allowed to say anything about this.' Later in the interview Dominitz admitted warily that the majority of Ethiopia's Jews had already entered Israel. It was common knowledge in Israel that thousands of Falashas were already there: they were visible for all to see. For some reason the publication of the *Nekuda* article was taken by two Israeli tabloids as marking the end of the embargo on the story, and on 3 January they ran front-page stories quoting Dominitz. As a result, Associated Press picked up the story, embroidered it with reports from elsewhere in the world and sent it off with explicit mention of the airlift. Immediately, the censors telephoned the Associated Press Tel Aviv office forbidding mention of the airlift. Associated Press tried to stop the story, claiming the Israeli paper *Ma'ariv* had been misquoted, but it was too late.

The most extraordinary feature of the leak is that the Israeli censors, who have the right to suppress any internal or external communications and who frequently exercise this right, failed to stop this story appearing in the first place in the Israeli press. There are those who have seen sinister forces at work here, but the most plausible explanation is that it was an oversight.

On the evening of 3 January, Prime Minister Peres decided that the government should confirm the story and a press conference was called for the following day. The government confirmation was all that was needed for the world's press to take up Operation Moses and turn it into one of the most sensational stories in recent times.

The press conference became the focus of recrimination between political groups within the Knesset. The Likkud threatened Peres with a commission of enquiry. Few people seemed to be satisfied by the government's argument that the press conference had been a last-ditch attempt to divert public attention from the rescue mission to the problems of absorption. US officials and many others believed that the operation could have continued for another two weeks as long as the Israeli government had held back its confirmation of the story. It has been claimed that Peres's decision to make a public statement originated in the inter-party rivalries of the ruling coalition government and that he wanted to take the credit for the operation before anyone else did. Darker suggestions have been made accusing Israel of deliberately bringing the airlift to a halt to prevent any more blacks from getting into the country. Neither argument is remotely persuasive.

On the other hand, the Prime Minister's attempt to 'focus attention where it should be and divert it from delicate aspects' was certainly not effective. It was also misguided because, as the *Jerusalem Post* put it, 'the press corps in Israel, or anywhere else, whether foreign or local, can't be channelled in such a manner'.

Even while the story was screaming from headlines all

round the world and dominating television and radio news broadcasts, all hope that the operation could continue had not been lost. On Friday, 4 January, Leon Dulzin, the man who more than any other had originated the leak, was asked on BBC Radio 4 if he regarded 'the leaking of the information at this point as being any sort of a disaster'. He replied: 'I wouldn't say a disaster. I would say it is a little risky. But I do believe that while the news came out in the open, very few will dare to stop it today, because it is such a great humanitarian operation that it would create an enormous scandal in the world if somebody would dare stop it.' The following day Sudan notified the United States that it would no longer be able to participate in the airlift and Operation Moses was dead.

The last TEA flight left Khartoum on 5 January under cover of darkness after the completion of the Jewish Sabbath. Only four more flights were needed to evacuate all the Ethiopian Jews from the refugee camps of Sudan.

CHAPTER NINE

Bravo Israel?

The media reaction in the West to the story of Operation Moses was extraordinary. In Britain the *Sunday Express* described the rescue of the Falashas as 'a triumph of the human soul ... by a great nation.... Israel alone ... was capable of plucking a whole people from the nightmare of the Ethiopian famine with such brilliant élan.' The *Daily Mail* carried the banner headlines: 'Rescue of the Lost Tribe.' 'Bravo Israel!' proclaimed the *Sun*, 'a real life adventure to match anything ever dreamed up by Hollywood.'

The serious British papers were no less congratulatory. The *Guardian*'s editorial ran:

There are no lengths to which Israel will not go to protect its people as in the raid on Entebbe, or to avenge them, as in the capture of Eichmann.... Israel makes its foreign policy on the hoof. If a job seems needed, do it now and talk about it later.... No other country would have had the nerve, and the total indifference to international niceties, to grab many thousands of people from the mountains of East Africa and fly them to another continent ... as a famine relief operation nothing could be more convincing than to gather up the victims and take them where there is plenty of food ... the governments which judge themselves responsible must do the best they can for their people. In this respect the Israelis have succeeded dramatically where the Ethiopians, over many years, have dramatically failed.

The *Guardian*'s leader contained a fair measure of equivocation as well as praise, as might be expected, but not so *The Times*:

The modern-day successors of Moses and Aaron found the authorities in the Sudan and Ethiopia more amenable than the Pharaoh was when they sought to lead out the so-called 'lost tribe' ... in its way as inspiring a story as the Biblical Exodus.... Israel, of course, was born in order to be a homeland for all the Jewish people, and so the welcome to the Falashas is in accordance with practice. But it is nevertheless an admirable action.

The *New York Times* made the telling point that 'for the first time in history thousands of black people are being brought into a country not in chains but as citizens'.

Television and radio made just as much of the story. A transcript of all major broadcasts in the United Kingdom covering the evacuation of the Ethiopian Jews to Israel between 3 and 11 January 1985 runs into hundreds of pages. The first reactions as expressed by ITV's 'News at Ten' were that the operation was 'proof of an extraordinary Jewish exodus and the lengths to which Israel will go to rescue the Jewish people'.

Western governments, in so far as they reacted at all, responded favourably to the news of Operation Moses. In Britain there were a number of hostile statements in the House of Commons. Mr Tony Marlow, a Conservative MP fearing that the Ethiopian Jews were to be used as 'front-line troops in the conquest of the West Bank', announced in the House that 'those of us who have seen at first hand the inhuman way the Palestinians are treated do not believe that the Falashas have been hijacked from their natural environment for humanitarian reasons'. Attacks were also made from the Labour benches; ignoring the fact that Israel had made generous contributions towards general famine relief in Ethiopia, Andrew Faulds accused the Jewish state of behaving in an exclusive fashion to the disregard of the rest of the Ethiopian population. The government's position, however, was made clear by Mr Richard Luce, Minister of State at the Foreign Office, who stated simply that the government believed that people had the right to move across frontiers if they wished to do so.

Inevitably, the US State Department reaction was soured by their anger that the operation had been prematurely halted because Israel had publicly acknowledged the airlift. One

Washington official was reported as saying: 'I can tell you
there is significant irritation in Washington. We stuck our
necks way out on this operation and Israel suddenly changes
the rules without consultation with us.'

Operation Moses was seen in many quarters in the United
States as essentially an American venture. The American
press, while lauding the operation, stressed the role played by
Sudan and the importance of American aid and diplomacy in
achieving Khartoum's agreement to the airlift.

The Jewish response throughout the world was naturally
one of euphoria. The plight of the black Jews had concerned
Jewish communities everywhere for many years. The *Jewish
Chronicle* declared, 'Once again Israel has given Jews cause for
pride', while the French *Tribune Juive* gave a similarly enthusiastic verdict: 'Operation Moses, like the Entebbe mission,
has again given every Jew throughout the world, not only the
hope but also the assurance that he is not isolated and that he
can count on Israel in every situation.'

Initial press response from black Africa was favourable, encouraging hopes in Jerusalem that Israel's African policies had
been given a useful boost. Hilary Ng'weno, the editor of the
Nairobi *Weekly Review*, called Operation Moses

One of those feats of international adventure for which the State of
Israel has now become well known ... a major reminder of Israel's
commitment to the unity of the Jewish nation and the fact that
Falashas are Africans cannot be ignored, even by anti-Israeli critics
who have in the past equated Zionism with racism.

Similar editorials resounded throughout the black African
world.

The extreme left wing naturally took a different view of the
story. The Trotskyist Workers' Revolutionary Party's daily
Newsline called the operation 'an Israeli stunt' and 'a cynical
and racist exploitation of starvation and misery ... a cover-up
for Zionist interest in crushing the Eritrean liberation struggle'. This line was taken by the Soviet Union in broadcasts to
the Arab world, although the internal Soviet mass media

avoided mentioning Operation Moses. One Moscow radio broadcast in Arabic complained: 'The Israeli operation to transport Ethiopian Jews to Israel was governed not by humanitarian motives but by a desire to exploit the natural disaster in Ethiopia ... they will be used to colonize occupied Arab territories ... as the gun muzzle of Israeli expansionists.' In other Eastern bloc countries the operation was given extensive local coverage. In Czechoslovakia, for instance, *Rude Pravo* reported indignantly and remarkably that

This action, labelled Operation Moses, cannot be considered anything other than a provocation as thousands of people have been moved without the agreement of their government ... this was not a matter of aid as the shameless government of Israel claims but a cynical abuse of victims of famine.

Israeli politicians must have been pleased with the public response in the West and hardly surprised by the reaction in the Soviet Union and elsewhere. But on this occasion it was the reaction in the Arab states and Ethiopia which was of most immediate relevance.

While Israel basked in the spotlight of world attention, President Numeiri squirmed. When news of the airlift broke within Sudan, it caused considerable anger. Wallposters were put up at Khartoum University denouncing Numeiri's collusion with the Zionist enemy and with the forces of American imperialism. A presidential adviser was quoted in the American press as admitting that the airlift had not proved 'very popular' with the Sudanese bureaucracy. None the less he dismissed the protests in the Arab world in a somewhat cavalier fashion by arguing that 'every Arab government had clandestine links with Israel'. Dissatisfaction with Numeiri's handling of critical issues such as the drought and the war in the south, as well as resentment in some quarters at the policy of Islamization, had created an ugly mood in Sudan and Numeiri's political future looked uncertain. After the military coup which deposed him in April, the collusion between Numeiri's *AmnulDawla* and Israel was highlighted. Former Prime Minister Sadiq el-Mahdi called for Numeiri to be charged with treason and stressed that, 'Anyone involved in the Falasha affair should be tried for high treason.'

The Arab states were not slow to denounce Sudan's obvious complicity in the evacuation of the Ethiopian Jews. On 5 January the Sudanese Ministry of Foreign Affairs issued the following statement, which made a spirited attempt to shift the blame:

Ethiopia has always been using the Ethiopian Jews as a bargaining card with Israel for obtaining arms and money through the Israeli Amiran Trading Company which is operating in Ethiopia and it is a well-known fact that Israel has been supplying Ethiopia with huge amounts of arms it has captured during its invasion of Southern Lebanon.... The Zionist Ethiopian plotting against Sudan is not a new one but it dates back to the early days of the independence of the Sudan.... Ethiopia is the only one responsible for its subjects and if anyone of these has found his way to Israel that has undoubtedly been made in collusion between Ethiopia and Israel.... The Sudan has always been dealing with the question of refugees, whose majority has come from Ethiopia, on humanitarian grounds and in accordance with the international conventions. It has continued sharing its bread with them and providing them with shelter and care in spite of the extra burden incurred upon the Sudan.

The statement concluded with a declaration of loyalty to the Arab cause: 'The Sudan need not reckon its unswerving positions and policies towards the Israeli enemy which is still occupying Palestine and other Arab territories.' In addition to this salvo of rhetoric, Sudan delivered a strongly worded rebuke to the American Ambassador in Khartoum. The United States had guaranteed discretion on their own and on Israel's behalf; but the Israeli government had publicly acknowledged that the airlift had taken place although, it must be said, the Israelis had been swift to deny that the Sudanese government had had anything to do with it.

Sudan's disclaimer of responsibility was not taken at its face value in the Arab world. Although the semi-official Egyptian paper *al-Ahram* gave Khartoum's denial some prominence and subsequently, with fraternal tact, ignored the topic, most other responses in the Muslim world were hostile. The Democratic

Front for the Liberation of Palestine asked for an Arab League boycott against Sudan. The PLO asked the Arab states to intervene and to request Numeiri to end the migration of the Falashas. A Kuwaiti paper roundly criticized the operation for its 'blatant racism and expansionism'. Libya's Colonel Gadaffi demanded an immediate extraordinary meeting of the Arab League, while Radio Tripoli reported that Sudan had been colluding with Israel and the United States for years and that 'since 1982 there have been contacts between the intelligence services of the USA and Sudan to concentrate Ethiopian Jews in areas in Sudan'. The Iranian Ministry of Foreign Affairs accused Numeiri of 'shamefully collaborating with the USA and Zionism to exploit the famine in Ethiopia to realize Israel's racist designs' while at the same time conspiring against Islam and betraying the Palestinian cause. The Jordanian paper *al-Dustur* was less direct and more ambivalent on the whole affair:

This daring, intelligent operation is undeniably another triumph for Zionism and Israel. But the important question is: Were Israeli boldness and intelligence the factors that made the operation possible, or was it the usual Arab weakness and stupidity or plotting on the part of others? Khartoum knows the answer. Let Khartoum speak!

Critical of the operation in much broader terms, *al-Ahram* complained: 'Famine does not distinguish between Jews and non-Jews. What Israel has done is save the Jews and leave the non-Jews dying.' The main and most frequently voiced Arab objection to the operation was best expressed by *al-Dustur*:

We are not against humanitarian initiatives towards people who are suffering or facing the threat of death. However, we oppose any assistance offered to certain people if this means oppressing another people. The Ethiopian Jews who were brought to Israel will replace other people who have been driven out of their homeland and who have been leading a life of pain and suffering in camps and exile for thirty-six years. These are the Palestinian people.

This position was adopted by a number of commentators throughout the world.

The media response in the Arab world was considerably more vigorous than any practical steps taken by Arab governments. Arab leaders were critical but no public censure of Sudan was made by the Arab League and no other measures were taken. The only reprisal was a recommendation by the Arab ambassadors in Brussels for a boycott of Trans European Airways. TEA's director, Georges Gutelman, was summoned to their meeting in order to explain his airline's role, but he refused to attend.

In Ethiopia, the Dergue's immediate response was to call for an end to 'this illegal and clandestine operation which is a gross interference in the internal affairs of Ethiopia'. The Ethiopian Foreign Ministry explained the airlift as a 'conspiracy between the Sudanese government and foreign powers in the illegal trafficking of Ethiopians from Sudanese territory to Israel and other countries'. Consequently, in a television interview with CBC, Colonel Mengistu Haile Mariam explained his objections to the exodus of the Falashas:

These people were forced from our territory, from parts of Ethiopia where we do not have very tight security. They were almost dragged against their will to go to Israel. The most astounding thing in this context is the fact that this particular case has for the first time prompted the Arabs and the Israelis to join against Ethiopia. This act is illegal and inhuman, and indeed it is an indirect form of slavery. The whole world knows the injustice to which the Jews have been subjected ... the Jews are now reversing the injustice and committing it against Ethiopians. The crushing fact is that the Falashas, in order to escape this situation, are now committing suicide simply to get out of the alien situation they have been forced into.

Suspicions have been voiced in some quarters that the Ethiopians turned a blind eye to the operation in exchange for arms. It is known that for some years Israel has been supplying Ethiopia with a variety of arms, particularly with spare parts for ageing American F5 fighter planes as well as with various Russian arms and parts which were captured in Southern Lebanon and which the Israelis are said to be selling more cheaply than the USSR. The fact that Israel has supplied Ethiopia with arms is not, according to the Institute of Strategic Studies, in doubt, but the likelihood of a trade-off is slight. In reality, it is unlikely that the Dergue, faced with the twin crises of famine and civil war, gave the Falashas any attention until Operation Moses hit the world's headlines. In any case, as Mengistu admitted, there are many northern and border areas of Gondar where the Ethiopian armed forces have little control. When Falashas had to move through army-controlled territory, they travelled fearfully at night and did their best to conceal their movements. There are no reports of the army's connivance in their escape. For the most part the Ethiopian government had not much more hope of being able to control the Falasha exodus than it had of preventing the exodus of hundreds of thousands of other refugees from Tigre and Eritrea over the last year.

Since the beginning of January 1985, the Addis Ababa newspapers have been full of rabidly anti-Semitic and anti-Zionist propaganda. Operation Moses is constantly characterized as an act of 'international piracy'. The Falashas, it is claimed, were kidnapped by Israeli agents and taken to Sudan against their will, and the press calls loudly for their return to Ethiopia. It is unlikely that this propaganda campaign will improve the lot of the Jews still in Ethiopia.

The future of the estimated 7–8,000 Falashas who remain is unclear. Many of them will undoubtedly want to join their families in Israel. They should be allowed to. The Ethiopian government should remember that Ethiopia has approved the Universal Declaration of Human Rights and the 1981 African Charter on Human and Peoples' Rights, which confirm that 'everyone has the right to leave any country, including his own'.

CHAPTER TEN

Operation Sheba

When Operation Moses came to an abrupt halt on 5 January
1985, Joshua and others involved in the operation were waiting anxiously in Khartoum for news of a group of Falasha
monks who had set off from Kwara, west of Lake Tana, and
who were expected to arrive at the Sudanese border, where
special arrangements had been made to meet them. The
Falasha agents of the Mossad who had been helping in the
arrangements for the airlift were particularly concerned for
the monks' safe arrival. Not only were these men highly respected by the Ethiopian Jewish community because of their
great sanctity, but the monks were bringing from their mon-
astery much of the Falasha literary heritage in the form of
ancient books and manuscripts.

The international reverberations caused by the leak of the
airlift resulted in the border with Gondar being closed from
both the Ethiopian and the Sudanese sides. The monks of
Kwara, like thousands of other Falashas who had been on
their way to Sudan and Israel, are now presumed trapped
somewhere in Ethiopia.

After the last TEA flights left Khartoum, there were thought
to be around 1,000 Falashas left in Sudan. Four more flights
would have cleared them. Those left behind were young, relatively fit people, many of whom had volunteered to stay on
to help organize the exodus. By this time, although there were
a few families in Um Raquba and Wad el Heluw, it was
thought that almost all the Ethiopian Jews in Sudan had been
concentrated in the staging-camp at Tewawa. Cut off from
news of their families in Israel, one can readily understand the
desperation felt by the Falashas in the camp. The hostile re-

action within Sudan to news of the airlift, as well as the envy of the wretched Christian and Muslim refugees who had witnessed the daily departures during November and December, made their situation even more precarious than it had been before.

They had not, however, been forgotten. In Israel, Prime Minister Peres promised that every available measure was being considered to bring out the Jews who had been left behind. In the United States and Canada, the AAEJ and the CAEJ continued their campaigns with renewed vigour. By now, the whole of the American Jewish community was deeply involved in the plight of the Falashas and the full weight of the community was put behind attempts to influence the American government to take action on behalf of their black brethren in Africa. US initiatives were not slow in coming. In early February two US senators, Dennis de Concini and Paul S. Trible, visited Jewish villages in Gondar and tried to assess the situation of the Falashas remaining in Ethiopia. Subsequently, they appealed to the Ethiopian authorities to permit the Falashas to emigrate freely in order to be reunited with their families in Israel. Unnamed Ethiopian officials were quoted in the American press as saying that they would 'seriously consider' the senators' proposals. A more authentic message of the intentions of the Dergue was delivered during the senators' visit when two Ethiopian members of the American delegation were beaten up by security officials shortly after a visit to a Jewish village. This was taken as a clear expression of the resentment felt by the Ethiopian government at the continuing American interest in the Falashas. In practical terms, the senators were unable to achieve any result as far as the Falashas went.

The pressure on the US government increased. In late February, President Reagan received individual letters from 100 senators urging him to use American influence to rescue at least those Falashas stranded in Sudan. Anxious, perhaps, to mollify Jewish voters, who had overwhelmingly voted against him in the November elections, Reagan decided to take action.

In the first week of March the American Vice-President, George Bush, visited Khartoum for meetings with Sudanese leaders. There were a number of outstanding issues between the two countries. The US government had decided to hold back £100 million of the funds Khartoum had been promised 'pending the Sudanese government's implementation of an economic reform package', in the words of a State Department spokesman. This led to a number of press reports throughout the world which, according to a State Department statement of 19 February, 'had provoked considerable misunderstanding, including the incorrect conclusion that there is a crisis in relations between the US and Sudan'.

If there was no crisis in US–Sudan relations, there was certainly a crisis in Sudan itself. Hundreds of thousands more Ethiopian refugees had crossed into east Sudan, the drought was threatening millions of Sudan's own people, the war in the south was continuing unabated, and Numeiri's political virtuosity and showmanship were fooling no one. The Sudanese crisis could only be solved with money. No organization in the world, including the IMF, was prepared to advance any more funds to Sudan until its existing debts had been paid off. Numeiri needed still more US money desperately.

The most immediate effect of Bush's 6 March meeting with Numeiri was to release $15 million of suspended aid. Following this, Numeiri gave his agreement in principle to a further airlift of Falashas out of Sudanese territory. There were three conditions: the Israelis should have nothing to do with it; it should be kept an absolute secret; and the flights should not go directly from Sudan to Israel. The airlift had the personal blessing of President Reagan.

A number of factors must have affected Numeiri's decision to go along with the scheme. In the first place, the international reaction to Operation Moses had been far less fierce than he might reasonably have feared and he had gained considerable credit from the Americans for going along with it; secondly, there was a good chance that this operation, which was to be planned and carried out within the space of a couple of weeks, could in fact be done clandestinely; and thirdly, Numeiri had no choice. Without more American aid he was finished.

Code-named Operation Sheba, the airlift of the remaining Falashas from Tewawa was planned by the CIA, the American State Department and the US air force. Falasha Mossad agents had the responsibility of ensuring that the Jews waiting in Tewawa were ready to leave and that they were indeed Falashas. It was a well-planned operation, which was conducted in total secrecy. Aid workers in Khartoum, who had been expecting some continuation of the Falasha emigration, were caught completely by surprise. A Khartoum-based diplomat was quoted by *The Times*: 'They've really kept the lid on this one. We hadn't heard even a whisper of it. We were expecting such a move but not yet. We thought they would wait much longer until the dust had settled after the last escapade.'

On the night of 28 March 1985, 481 Falashas were taken under cover of darkness by trucks from Tewawa to an airstrip eight miles north of Gedaref. Six American air force Turbo-prop C130 transport planes painted in desert camouflage, which had flown from an American base near Frankfurt, landed at twenty-minute intervals at the desert strip. High winds delayed the operation, which was not completed until 9 a.m.

The Falashas had been issued with visas for European destinations in order to comply with President Numeiri's condition that there should be no direct flight from Sudan to Israel. None the less, it is believed that the planes flew directly from Gedaref to the Israeli air force base at Rimon in the Negev desert.

The secrecy of the operation was not maintained. By a too remarkable coincidence Charles Powers, the Nairobi correspondent of the *Los Angeles Times*, happened to be in the desert outside Gedaref on the morning of the airlift, witnessed everything and filed his eye-witness account which was duly published. After the disclosure of Operation Sheba, speculation was rife in Khartoum that Powers had been tipped off by the Americans. Subsequently, Powers wrote a long article for the

Los Angeles Times giving the total credit for masterminding the earlier operation, Operation Moses, to an official in the US embassy, who was awarded a citation during Vice-President Bush's visit to Sudan. Although the American reporter gave no names, the embassy official referred to was clearly Jerry Weaver, the refugee co-ordinator, who while not the 'mastermind' of the operation had certainly played a vital role in Operation Moses as well as the emigration of Falashas which had preceded it.

The Sudanese condition of secrecy had not been met, but no great harm was done. There was little international reaction to Operation Sheba and, indeed, the idea of Falashas leaving Sudan in dramatic circumstances had become such a commonplace that there were those who could not understand why Numeiri wanted to keep the affair secret at all. The *New York Times* wrote: 'President Numeiri of Sudan wanted no publicity for a simple act of decency – permitting the United States to airlift 800 [*sic*] stranded Ethiopian Jews to Israel. He deserves much credit for going ahead with the decision, but it is appalling that he felt compelled to play down so modest a gesture.'

At about the same time that the American air force was taking out the Falashas from Gedaref, more discreet means were being used to transport the rest of the Jews who had been stranded in Sudan. Using regular international flights out of Khartoum, another several hundred Falashas were flown to Israel. Tewawa was now cleared and it was thought that the Sudan operation was over.

Unknown to the organizers of Operation Sheba and the various agencies in Khartoum who had facilitated the rest of the Falashas' departure, there had been further developments. At the beginning of January, Metemma, Abderafi and Humera, the main crossing-points from the Gondar region into Sudan, had been closed on both sides of the border. Many Falashas were reportedly trapped in areas close to the frontier. But some of them had been travelling into Sudan through a long and circuitous route through rebel-held parts of Tigre and Eritrea. In January 1985 the Oxford University Medical

Officer, Dr Bent Juel-Jensen, visited Sudan on behalf of Ethiopian Aid. In his written account, he recorded visiting Wad Sherifat, a refugee camp near Kassala, where he found 35,000 Ethiopians in dreadful circumstances. Among them he discovered a group of 165 Falashas, who had just arrived from Begemder. They had crossed the Semien mountains and had been travelling for many weeks. Their condition was dire. There was not enough food, not enough medicine and the 'housing' was virtually non-existent: '... the shelters for the newly arrived refugees are of the most primitive kind built with straw from sorghum and a few sticks, nothing like the more solidly built gojos [*tukuls*] in Um Raquba....' In addition to the newly arrived group, there were at least another 1,000 Falashas in the camp. His report states that while he was there sixty Falashas were dying every day from malaria, measles and starvation. The appalling death rate among the Falashas was very much higher than that in the camp as a whole, where 'twenty to thirty-three' non-Falashas were dying every day. Juel-Jensen believes that this is because the Falashas had travelled much further than the other refugees and had suffered terrible deprivations on the way. Unlike the Eritrean and Tigrean refugees, they had no rebel-organized feeding-stations to rely on during their journey into Sudan. With the collapse of Operation Moses, the Mossad support system had been effectively destroyed. Starving, disease-ridden and frightened of their neighbours, the Falashas in Wad Sherifat face an uncertain future.

By the end of February the restrictions on the Sudan–Ethiopian border near Gedaref were relaxed and thereafter straggling groups of Falashas were seen heading for Um Raquba. By the beginning of June there were over fifty Jews in the camp and dozens more had made their way to Tewawa. What will become of these people? It is to be hoped that the new regime in Khartoum will permit the Falashas already in Sudan to leave. Their situation, particularly in Wad Sherifat, is critical and those whose responsibility it is to rescue them and get them to Israel should not tarry. Graenum Berger, now in retirement, will no doubt ensure that they do not.

CHAPTER ELEVEN

Israel

I became a Zionist on the day I fled with my mother from the Budapest ghetto and there was nowhere for us to hide. They wanted to kill us and in the whole world there was nowhere for us to go. We had to return to the ghetto but since then I have known that there has to be a place somewhere on the face of the earth which can offer haven to a Jewish child whose life is threatened by Nazis or by famine. In one sentence that is what Zionism is. Welcome my black brothers. You are helping us to understand what we are doing here.

Yosef Lapid's editorial in *Ma'ariv* expressed in personal terms the feelings of most Israelis in the heady days of January that followed the news of the airlift. A holiday atmosphere seemed to pervade the whole country and with it a renewal of national pride and a confirmation of Israel's essential purpose in the world: to be a shelter for Jews in distress. The fastidious attitude adopted by the religious authorities, before and after Operation Moses, was angrily attacked everywhere. 'They have more right to be here than most of us because they have suffered on account of their Judaism and many of us have not', protested one Israeli paper. The operation was a success story, which was badly needed to bolster national morale at a time of economic crisis and amid the tragedy of Israel's continuing involvement in Lebanon. It also did something for Israel's flagging immigration. Considered by the independent newspaper *Ha-Aretz* as 'one of the most brilliant Israeli enterprises in the area of immigration', Operation Moses inspired the editor of the left-wing *Al-Ha-Mishmar* to reflect: 'How sweet it is sometimes to breathe the perfume of victory – a victory of the Zionist ideal!'

Angered by Arab criticism of the 'splendid' airlift, Israel's

President, Chaim Herzog, retorted that the Arab states could have alleviated the misery of the refugees for whom *they* had a moral responsibility – the Palestinians – with just one day's oil revenues, but they chose not to. The fact that Israel cared for its own was a source of pride to everyone. But it was a particularly proud day for Israel's President for other reasons. Eleven years before, as Israel's Ambassador to the United Nations, Herzog had torn up the UN Zionism is racism resolution on the floor of the General Assembly. The arrival of the black Jews in such numbers would surely confirm, if anything ever would, the pointlessness of that odious resolution.

For some time before the story of the airlift became public, thousands of Israelis who had heard what was happening had waited every night, often in torrential rain, to greet the Falashas as they arrived dressed in their filthy rags at Ben-Gurion Airport. The sight of the black Jews kneeling to kiss the soil of the Holy Land reminded many of an almost lost idealism. An Israeli military correspondent told me: 'I saw an old man get off the plane. He looked around in bewilderment and walked across the tarmac to a group of palm trees just in front of the arrivals hall. He prostrated himself and began to eat the soil clinging to the base of the tree. Seeing that made me feel different about this bloody country.'

Money, clothes and toys for the new immigrants poured in from the Israeli public. The Israel Dental Association undertook to provide free dental care for the newcomers. Building contractors in some cases offered to renovate apartments free of charge for the Ethiopians. Thousands of young people volunteered for the task of teaching the Falashas Hebrew, while thousands more offered to adopt the orphans who had come in with the operation. The kibbutz movement immediately announced that the kibbutzim would welcome as many Falashas as cared to come. Throughout the country, for a few days at least, there was a sense of participating in a new and glorious chapter of the national pageant. People recalled the early days of the state when wave after wave of refugees had come from the Yemen, from the squalid *mellahs* of Morocco and the displaced persons camps of post-war Europe. As

Ma'ariv put it, 'there was a sense of re-living days long gone, a sense of history knocking on our door'.

Unfortunately, there were other reactions too. Zionism is not racism, but some Israelis are racist and expressions of unfriendliness and bigotry soon made themselves felt. The mayor of Eilat, in a much publicized statement, said that he only wanted Falashas to settle in his resort town if they could 'sing and dance and be useful for entertaining the tourists'. A few development town mayors refused to take Falashas because of the high unemployment rates in their areas. But there were other reasons for not taking them as well: Barukh Almakiyas, head of the district council of Yeruham, a shabby little desert town not far from the Dead Sea, refused even to consider taking Falashas 'in their present state'. Throughout the country patronizing and exaggerated accounts circulated about how primitive the Falashas were. Stories were passed around with relish of the Ethiopians putting their shoes in the fridge and washing themselves in the lavatory, or failing to nego-tiate stairs or door handles with which they were unfamiliar. Dubbed 'stone-age primitives', they were thought by some never to have come into contact with cars, stairs, electricity or running water. They were accused of being dirty and knowing nothing of dental hygiene (although the Falashas have enviable teeth and have their own methods of keeping them clean). At one middle-class dinner-party, a woman was heard welcom-ing the arrival of the Falashas on the grounds that they would provide a new source of cheap maids and house helps.

Somewhat patronizing attitudes were also adopted by some well-meaning liberals who, in incredulous tones, were heard extolling the extraordinary intelligence of the black Jews, their adaptability and capacity for hard work. In some circles the Falashas seemed set to become the new Yemenites, who for years had been the 'oriental' Jewish group most favoured by the Ashkenazi establishment.

As soon as the Falashas arrived in Israel, they were taken under the wing of the Jewish Agency. They were all given intensive medical examinations and kept under close medical surveillance for the first several weeks. Issued with new clothes, shoes, watches and baggage, they were dispersed in family groups to a dozen or so absorption centres run by the Agency throughout the country. Each family was given an apartment, and for the next year they could look forward to being attended and supervised by teams of trained social workers, teachers and medical staff while they acquired a knowledge of Hebrew and the other skills necessary for them to cope with Israeli life. Veteran Falasha immigrants play an important part in the process and act as intermediaries and interpreters in the absorption centres. No one who has seen a centre in action can fail to be impressed by the devotion and competence of the staff and the eagerness of the Falashas to take advantage of what is being offered them. The Immigration and Absorption Department of the Jewish Agency, led by Chaim Aron, made a magnificent contribution to their integration. There is probably no country in the world where new immigrants are given such a good start.

Considerable international controversy was provoked by the decision to send one small group of some sixty Falasha families to Kiryat Arba on the Israeli-occupied West Bank. Whereas this move demonstrated no great political acumen on the part of the Jewish Agency, it hardly confirms the suspicions expressed by a number of journalists that the entire objective of Operation Moses was to provide settlers for the West Bank.

It is now acknowledged that much of the rich cultural heritage of earlier immigrants to Israel was lost through a misguided but natural desire on the part of policy-makers to create a homogeneous national culture. The Israelis seem determined to avoid making the same mistake this time. Attempts are already being made to preserve and foster aspects of Falasha culture in Israel. Workshops are being set up in Safed to enable Falasha potters to carry on with their ancient craft. Falasha weaving, embroidery and metalwork are being encouraged. There are already troupes of Falasha singers and dancers touring the country. Amharic–Hebrew dictionaries have been produced and there is talk of establishing an Amharic language radio channel. Clearly there is a limit to how far the Falashas can be directed in this respect, and quite what these initiatives will achieve is open to question. In fact, there are already signs that the younger Falashas are anxious to remove all vestiges of their former life and to to assimilate as thoroughly as they can to Israeli mores. There is little chance that the Falasha religion will survive in Israel. Already the Falashas are being required to assimilate to 'normative' Judaism and they seem happy to do so.

The initial prejudice that the Falashas encountered in Israel, limited as it was, caused understandable resentment among them. One teenage boy said: 'We the black Jews are happy that there are white Jews but I am not so sure that all of the white Jews are happy that there are black Jews.' I spoke to one Falasha who had worked as a water engineer in Addis Ababa. Wearing the good quality dark blue anorak which was standard issue to all the Falashas, he complained in fluent English: 'They don't need me here – their water techniques are different and my skills cannot be applied. We are parasites here, all of us. We want to help Israel and contribute to the state but we are holding them back. We're parasites. And some of the workers here make us feel like parasites.'

Colonel Mengistu has claimed that the Falashas in Israel have been traumatized by the racist attitudes they have encountered. This is nonsense. The greatest source of unhappiness among the Falashas in Israel is their recent past. The traumas of their flight from Ethiopia, the months of waiting in the camps in Sudan, bereavement and separation are the factors which affect them most.

An Israeli psychiatrist told me that one Falasha girl had been raped several times by a group of *shiftas* a few miles from the Sudanese border. When she arrived at the refugee camp in Sudan, Falasha notions of purity and chastity had caused the young woman to be disowned by her family. She became fair game for the young Falasha men who treated her like a whore. When the woman arrived in Israel, the young Falashas in the absorption centre continued treating her in the same way. She was harassed mercilessly. Seeing what was happening, an Israeli social worker put her in a centre in another part of the country, but it was not long before the Falashas there found out about the woman and the process started again. Eventually the girl suffered a nervous breakdown and is now an in-patient in a psychiatric hospital in Beersheba. Another Falasha left his native village in Gondar with his wife and three children. Two of the children and his wife died on the way to Sudan. Shortly after the man's arrival in Israel, unbalanced by grief, he was found trying to strangle his surviving daughter. He is also in the Beersheba psychiatric hospital. Two hundred and fifty-six Falasha children arrived in Israel without either parent. Many of the parents did not survive the journey to Sudan, whilst others had died in the refugee camps; some have perhaps found their way back to Ethiopia. The tragic events touch them all. Ora Danyo, a senior official at the Jewish Agency, has said: 'There is not a family that has not lost someone from hunger, disease or other calamity on the way here.'

The Falashas reserved their greatest fury for those journalists and officials they considered responsible for leaking the news of the first airlift. Yeshayahu, a Falasha who had come to Israel from Gondar a year before, expressed his views to the *Jerusalem Post*: 'What Dulzin said was bad. Now everyone knows. All the families are stopped on the way. The airlift will not start again. Now they'll die. Only God can help.' Rahamim Elazar, head of the Public Council for Ethiopian Jewry, claimed that the Jewish Agency had conspired with the Israeli government to sabotage the operation because they did not want the problem of assimilating the thousands of Falashas who were still in Africa. Many of the Falashas were encouraged by the AAEJ to be suspicious of the government and to question its integrity.

The demand by the orthodox establishment that the Ethiopian Jews undergo some form of ritual conversion is perhaps the greatest obstacle to the Falashas feeling welcome in their new country. 'When will you let us feel that we have really come home?' asked a Falasha leader at a recent meeting with Israel's two chief rabbis, Avraham Shapira (Ashkenazi) and Mordekhai Eliahu (Sephardi).

Ever since Chief Rabbi Ovadia Yosef's 1973 ruling, the

Falashas who have made their way to Israel have had to undergo a symbolic conversion, known as a 'conversion in doubt', to put an end to any lingering question that might arise as to their Jewishness. This process involves three elements: circumcision (*mila*), ritual immersion (*tevila*), and a general declaration of willingness to keep the commandments (*kabbalat ol mitzvot*). Like other Jews, Falasha males are circumcised on the eighth day after birth; but because it was feared that their circumcision might not have been entirely in accordance with orthodox Jewish practice, it was decided to apply a symbolic circumcision which involves taking a drop of blood from the penis and reciting the appropriate blessings. At the beginning of December 1984, however, under pressure from all sides, the rabbinate dropped the requirement of 'conversion' and with it the symbolic circumcision, which had caused great offence to Ethiopians and to the great majority of Israelis. Amos Elon, the distinguished Israeli writer and journalist, said to me with characteristic indignation: 'We have the nerve to call *them* primitive when the first thing we do when they arrive is to take a drop of blood from their penis!'

Symbolic circumcision is no longer demanded, but the other basic requirements are in force, although a growing number of orthodox rabbis in Israel are prepared to ignore them. Rather than 'conversion', the new ceremony is called 'renewal of the covenant'. The orthodox argument now is that since the Falashas had been cut off from the main body of Jewry for so long, there may have been irregularities in matters such as marriage and divorce which could have permitted the admixture of non-Jews into the tribe, particularly since the Falashas' conversion rights differed. To obviate any such doubts, the rabbis are still insisting upon immersion and the declaration of acceptance of the commandments. Chief Rabbi Avraham Shapira stated his views thus: 'It is our interest that this community be absorbed within the people of Israel in its entirety. We wish to prevent the stigma of a separate tribe – "not real members of the Jewish people" – and to prevent the possibility of serious problems concerning their individual status as Jews.' Here as elsewhere, the rabbis' legalistic approach to who is a Jew leaves little room for graciousness or mitigating circumstances. Their stance has provoked widespread dismay in Israel and abroad, but would have little relevance for anyone outside orthodox circles were it not for the fact that it is the orthodox rabbinate which is responsible for determining who is a Jew and consequently who can become an Israeli.

'We are the Jews who have paid the highest price in all the world to come to Jerusalem and yet we are treated differently from the white Jews', complained one Falasha. Rabbi Yosef HaDani, the first ordained rabbi from among the Falashas, has expressed the affront felt by the Ethiopian Jews: 'This is not a humane approach. It is a terrible shame to do this in the name of Judaism. It is a blight on the Torah itself to cast doubt on the community in this manner.' The Falashas are right. It is a disgrace that a people who have suffered persecution in countless forms for generations should have to undergo what they consider a humiliating procedure in order to become what they think they already are.

There is, however, nothing very new about the Falashas' predicament and nothing in the rabbis' objections that can be termed racism. A number of groups, including American Reform Jews wishing to marry Israelis and the Bene Israel Jews of India, have had similar problems. Even the old Ashkenazi establishment is not immune. David Ben-Gurion's son Amos served in the British army during the Second World War and married an Englishwoman, who converted to Judaism. Their daughter, the grand-daughter of the first and most illustrious prime minister of the Jewish state, the George Washington of Israel, had to go through the ceremony of immersion and symbolic conversion before she could marry under Jewish law. The problem is this: as long as the Israeli rabbinate is left to determine who is a Jew, the liberal definitions, shared by most Israelis, of what constitutes Jewishness can never be applied.

To most Jews outside orthodox circles the plea of Habtnesh Ezra contains something of a moral imperative:

We the Ethiopian Jews have secluded ourselves from gentiles and
gentile customs far more than any other Jewish community to avoid
dilution of our Jewishness. We have struggled against all odds to
preserve our faith and carry out the Torah to the extent of sacrificing
our lives. And until reunification with world Jewry, we thought we
were the only remaining Jews in the world, yet we continued to be
diligent in our observance of the Torah. We demand fairness and
equality: one is either a Jew or not a Jew. This humiliation must
stop once and for all. Ethiopian Jews deserve to be respected as Jews
returning to their homeland like any other Jewish community.

A growing body of opinion within the bastion of orthodoxy
is unhappy about the rulings made on the Falashas' status. At
the beginning of March 1985, former Chief Rabbis Ovadia
Yosef and Shlomo Goren declared that the Ethiopian Jews
should be accepted as full Jews without the need for any
additional ceremony. It is probable that in time the Falashas
will win this last battle for full recognition.

The Falashas' arrival in Israel has been somewhat marred
by the rabbinate's insensitivity. None the less, there is no
doubt that they are glad to be in Israel. Many of the Falashas
I met were radiant with happiness and profoundly grateful
for everything that was being done for them. There are already signs that their integration into Israeli society will be
successful. In Jerusalem I met a handsome young Falasha who
told me he planned to marry soon. I asked him if he would
marry a Falasha girl. 'No,' he replied, 'most of us want to
marry white girls. It is not good that there are white Jews and
black Jews. We will marry them and they will marry us. In
two or three generations there will be no more Falashas.'

In the meantime, the community will have many problems
as they adapt to Israeli life and face up to the future which
their faith and courage have secured for them. As they left
Gondar, this ancient Falasha prayer must have been on many
minds:

Hear our prayer, God, King of the Universe,
When you help your people, Israel,
You help all mankind.
Have mercy on the city of Jerusalem.
Let us enjoy your kingdom
With your chosen people in Israel.

Select Bibliography

Kessler, David, *The Falashas: The Forgotten Jews of Ethiopia* (George Allen & Unwin, London, 1982)

Leslau, Wolf (ed. and trs.), *Falasha Anthology: The Black Jews of Ethiopia* (Schocken, New York, 1969)

Parfitt, Tudor, and Kessler, David, *The Falashas* (Minority Rights Group Report No. 67, London, 1985)

Rappoport, L., *The Lost Jews: Last of the Ethiopian Falashas* (Stein & Day, New York, 1980)

Ullendorff, Edward, *The Ethiopians* (Oxford University Press, London, 1965)

Ullendorff, Edward, *Ethiopia and the Bible* (published for the British Academy by Oxford University Press, London, 1968)